BEYOND BACKYARD
ENVIRONMENTALISM

"New Democracy Forum operates at a level of literacy and responsibility which is all too rare in our time." —John Kenneth Galbraith

BEYOND BACKYARD ENVIRONMENTALISM

CHARLES SABEL, ARCHON FUNG, AND BRADLEY KARKKAINEN

FOREWORD BY HUNTER LOVINS AND AMORY LOVINS

EDITED BY JOSHUA COHEN AND JOEL ROGERS
FOR *BOSTON REVIEW*

BEACON PRESS
BOSTON

BEACON PRESS
25 Beacon Street
Boston, Massachusetts 02108-2892
www.beacon.org

Beacon Press books
are published under the auspices of
the Unitarian Universalist Association of Congregations.

05 04 03 02 01 00   8 7 6 5 4 3 2 1

This book is printed on acid-free paper that contains at least 20
percent postconsumer waste and meets the uncoated paper ANSI/NISO
specifications for permanence as revised in 1992.

Composition by Wilsted & Taylor Publishing Services

Library of Congress Cataloging-in-Publication Data

Sabel, Charles.
    Beyond backyard environmentalism / Charles Sabel, Archon Fung, and
    Bradley Karkkainen / foreword by Hunter Lovins and Amory Lovins ; edited
    by Joshua Cohen and Joel Rogers for *Boston Review*.
        p. cm.—(New democracy forum)
    ISBN 0-8070-0445-6 (pa)
    1. Environmental policy.   2. Environmental protection.
    3. Social responsibility of corporations.   I. Cohen, Josh.
    II. Rogers, Joel.   III. Series.
    GE170.B49   2000
    363.7'05765—dc21

                                        00-023727

CONTENTS

3

FOREWORD

HUNTER LOVINS AND AMORY LOVINS

Wouldn't you prefer to live in a world that didn't need regulations to protect the environment? This book describes the first steps to achieve that goal. In such a world, businesses would be accountable to their communities and would eliminate waste to enhance profits. Natural resources like forests would be valued on corporate balance sheets as habitat and watershed as well for the board feet of timber they contain. The integrity of coral reefs would count as much as the cost of production. Federal regulations would be not-so-quaint anachronisms of the last millennium.

A wild utopian vision? Not at all. In fact, this world is slowly emerging. Our latest work with Paul Hawken, *Natural Capitalism: Creating the Next Industrial Revolution*, describes some of the many companies that are already realizing that they can gain competitive advantage by going beyond compliance to become sustainable and even restorative enterprises. A growing number of corporate leaders have realized that sustainability is both a personal commitment and a business imperative.

We have sat in meetings of a number of companies whose senior management is more ardently committed to doing the right thing than the most zealous environmental activist. They are redesigning how they do business not just to minimize waste, but to eliminate any toxicity in their processes, because they know they will make more money in this way, and because it is the future that they want for their company, for their children, and for the world. These executives are inventing the next Industrial Revolution, whose hallmark will be dramatically reduced environmental impacts because they use resources one hundred times more productively, because they take their values from their customers, their discipline from the market, and their model from nature.

Until all businesses behave this way, however, regulation will be a fact of life. But it could sure be done more effectively. Businesspeople and environmentalists alike are frustrated with federally imposed, centrally organized, remotely enforced rules and regulations. Despite the honest hopes of the early advocates that they could mandate protection of the environment, most of the real problems can't be solved through legislation, regulation, and litigation. Governments, in short, commonly lack the local knowledge of problems that is needed for their efficient solution. And even when they have the knowledge, their actions are often compromised or derailed by the pleadings of special interests.

Tip O'Neill once said that all politics is local. He could have added that most environmental problems are, too, and should be solved by people with local expertise. National, cookie-cutter laws frustrate companies, and rarely solve the problem at hand. Managers do as little as they think they can get away with; overworked, understaffed regulators have to rely on mechanistic policies; and the environment continues to deteriorate. And that's the bottom line: we have a lot of sympathy for managers trying to do a job in a morass of red tape, and for the regulators trying to save something of nature in a world that seems bent on destroying anything that doesn't add to the current quarter's profits. But mostly we care about the environment that continues to degrade. Clinging to rigid positions isn't meeting the challenge.

This book offers a middle ground. Solutions to what are inherently local issues are more likely to be found through more flexible approaches like collaborative decision making and whole-system thinking by people who are directly affected. The book offers practical insights and useful case studies. It describes the future of environmental regulation. As Charles Sabel, Archon Fung, and Bradley Karkkainen show, environmental progress can be made sensibly, by setting appropriate standards and monitoring performance relative to them, rather than just complying minimally with outdated prescriptive requirements. They also illustrate a system that encourages broad "ownership" of the process and results by a wide range of stakeholders. And funny thing: when people are invested and involved they are more likely to follow through and hold each other accountable, which increases the likelihood of actual progress.

Sabel, Fung, and Karkkainen call for a "rolling-rule regime," a new style of regulation applicable in the first instance to environmental policies, but ultimately of wider interest. Taking the limits on centralized solutions as a point of departure, they propose a new regime that would permit more decentralized and varied solutions to problems while encouraging broad participation in the process and ownership of the results by a wide range of stakeholders. Properly executed, the rolling-rule regime will bring gains both in efficiency and democracy. More fully enlisting the capacities and knowledge of local actors increases efficiency. Enhancing our collective capacity to achieve desirable social goals, and more widely involving and educating citizens to foster such achievement all lie at the heart of real democracy.

These are large claims, and the respondents to Sabel, Fung, and Karkkainen pose hard questions. Won't the decentralized regime proposed by these authors demand too much of ordinary citizens? Who gets included in the proposed deliberations, and how is that decided? What is the appropriate role of experts in all this? Can the model handle problems bigger than local ones? What's the hard legal framework that will organize and provide legitimacy for the many discussions? And, at the bottom line, does rolling-rule regulation really produce good results? While agreeing that, under the right conditions, a more deliberative, decentralized, and experimental regulatory style can help the environment, their critics wonder about whether those conditions really hold. Maybe, in the world as it is, traditional "command and control" techniques still have a place.

Good questions produce lively debate—and this is an important one. By delivering this message strongly, Sabel, Fung, and Karkkainen force evaluation of current practice and the consideration of alternatives while breaking out of the conventional "market" or "hierarchy" box. There has long been a lack of perceived alternatives in environmental governance. The choices offered in American public policy are often equally unappealing and unrealistic: unfettered markets operating with no social standards, or public hierarchies commanding our behavior. The kind of regulation proposed here suggests that that we can have both standards and flexibility, common norms and local experimentation in how to achieve them. That message is hopeful, but not naïve—especially given the huge variation and complexity of our environmental problems, and the ageless American dedication to pragmatism and local control.

The approaches offered in this book are a better way to move businesses in the direction of true corporate responsibility, especially those companies that have not yet realized that business cannot long endure on a dead planet. They are most robust, adaptive, and creative than the one-size-fits-all model that preceded them. And they are also more likely to succeed.

The real value of this book is not only that its thesis is correct, a rarity in itself. More, it offers the thesis *and* its critics. You get to decide which makes most sense. A bold commitment to experiments and new ways of thinking about how we might save this earth is long overdue. If you care about the environment, you need to be in on this debate.

EDITORS' PREFACE

JOSHUA COHEN AND JOEL ROGERS

Any central government's knowledge of the society it regulates is limited, and that limitation commonly diminishes
the achievement of democratic ideals. It can keep harmful
activity outside the reach of public correction ("underregulation"), or result in wasteful expenditure of public
resources in the enforcement of unnecessarily restrictive
mandates ("overregulation"). The problem is particularly
pronounced in those areas where understanding problems
requires detailed local knowledge and solutions require cooperation among conflicting actors.

But if such problems of centralized "command and control" regulation are apparent, no less are those of more local
or voluntary regulatory regimes. These often fail to address
problems at the needed scale, encourage destructive parochialism, or lead to no real action at all.

Drawing from recent experience in environmental regulation, Charles Sabel, Archon Fung, and Bradley Karkkainen believe we can square this circle and achieve governance that combines "the virtues of localism and
decentralization with the discipline of national coordination." Their proposal is a "rolling-rule regime," which
would give local actors more power to define and solve prob-

lems. Federal agencies would still monitor habitats and enforce standards, but their function would increasingly be
defined as one of pooling the lessons of diverse local experi-
ment. And, through cross-site benchmarking, those lessons
would increasingly constitute the content of standards
themselves. The result, our lead authors claim, will be "regulation that is more effective than current arrangements,
and more democratic."

Many of their respondents are not so confident. They
variously doubt the bottom-line efficacy of such regulation,
the feasibility of its required increase in citizen involvement, the legitimacy of its process, and the realism of its assumptions about power and consensus. But few doubt that
current regulation, even in areas of almost universal popular
concern, often suffers from the problems that "rolling rule"
seeks to address—and thus limits our shared capacity to
identify, and enforce, the democratic will.

1

BEYOND BACKYARD ENVIRONMENTALISM

CHARLES SABEL, ARCHON FUNG,
AND BRADLEY KARKKAINEN

While totemic species like the gray wolf and ecosystems of otherworldly beauty like Florida's Everglades grab the national spotlight, much of the painstaking work of endangered species protection, and environmentalism generally, is carried out in obscurer locales, on behalf of less-celebrated creatures. One of these is the Coachella Valley fringe-toed lizard, a small, three-eyed reptile that lives only in a harsh stretch of desert in Riverside County, California, that is threatened by development sprawling outward from Los Angeles. Even where its habitat remains, the lizard struggles for survival, able to live only in windblown sand that is neither too coarse nor too fine.

Efforts to save the lizard began in the late 1970s in a fierce, familiar battle between environmentalists and developers. Local environmentalists formed the Lizard Advisory Committee (or simply, the Lizard Club) and scored first by getting the species listed as endangered by state and federal agencies in 1980. But development continued and more desert habitat was destroyed until 1982, when environmentalists threatened to sue developers unless they replaced all of the acreage they destroyed with habitat suitable for the lizard. Developers balked and threatened to use their funds for protracted legal combat instead. When both sides realized that these strategies would lead them to gamble their futures on the vagrant jurisprudence of the Endangered Species Act, they turned to compromise, stepped beyond conventional approaches of environmental protection, and created a novel system of habitat management and species protection.

This innovation was the 1986 Coachella Valley habitat conservation plan (called the CVFTLHCP), the second of its type to be signed. Environmental groups, developers, and a cluster of local units of government agreed, under the supervision of the U.S. Fish and Wildlife Service (FWS), to set aside more than fifteen thousand acres in the lizard's habitat as a preserve. In return for withdrawing entirely from this preserve, developers were granted a waiver of strict provisions of the Endangered Species Act that would have prohibited them from building anywhere within the habitat of the fringe-toed lizard. In addition, the environmental groups, developers, and local governments agreed to monitor the lizard's condition.

Today, nearly fifteen years later, the fringe-toed lizard is still struggling to survive: Recent evaluations show that the preserve is less effective than it long appeared, and new habitat restoration measures will be necessary.[1] But the innovative combination of local goal setting and publicly accessible monitoring elaborated in the CVFTLHCP remains the lizard's best hope of survival, providing the necessary stream of timely, detailed data and operational flexibility to adjust conservation measures as conditions warrant.

The effort to save the fringe-toed lizard reverberated beyond the small patch of California desert where it began. More than 450 habitat conservation plans (HCPs) are now either in operation or in development nationally, and Coachella Valley has become a model for building them. Beyond species protection, activists and government agencies facing diverse challenges such as watershed management, ecosystem restoration, and industrial toxics have begun to overcome old antagonisms in favor of similar cooperative environmental problem solving.

This new approach grows out of a proud tradition of backyard environmentalism in which local activists—from Pacific Northwest forests, to Woburn and Love Canal, to California deserts—fought to reclaim authority over their lived environment. These pioneers of citizen environmental activism typically sought to keep harmful activity out of their neighborhoods and beloved lands—hence the acronym NIMBY for Not In My Backyard. In their struggles to protect themselves and their children from poisoned air, soil, and water, ordinary citizens have often pitted themselves against certified experts from corporations, government, and even big environmental organizations.

Recent developments such as the CVFTLHCP go beyond this earlier generation in two ways. First, citizens now face the daunting task of determining what should occur in their backyards: What kinds of activity are productive yet acceptably sustainable? Second, determining what the tolerable activities are, given continuous change in the nature of risks and our understanding of how to respond to them, requires them to transform their traditionally antagonistic relationships with experts into partnerships for environmental protection. For complex challenges like saving the fringe-toed lizard or preventing pollution without job losses often demand lasting and adaptable alliances that engage both the broad experience of professional practitioners and the contextual intelligence that only citizens possess. If the lesson of the first generation of backyard environmentalism was that citizens living in threatened communities, near polluting firms, or drawing on contaminated watersheds would not be overrun by distant corporate and governmental bureaucracies, the experience of the succeeding generation teaches that citizens with their new allies can fundamentally reshape regulatory systems.

This relationship is founded on an exchange between local units—such as the Lizard Club, neighbors on the same tributary planning together to reduce the polluting runoff from their farms, or a team of workers and managers planning to reduce the use and leakage of toxics in their plant—

and higher level authorities—a field office of the U.S. Fish and Wildlife Service, a state department of the environment, or a regional or national office of the Environmental Protection Agency (EPA). Within broad limits the local units set their own environmental performance targets and devise the means to achieve them. In return, they provide detailed reports on actual performance and possible improvements to overarching public authorities. The resulting framework replaces central command regulation with a combination of local experimentation and centralized pooling of experience. In this new architecture—we will call it a rolling-rule regime—regulators use reports on proposals and outcomes to periodically reformulate minimum performance standards, desirable targets, and paths for moving from the former to the latter. While pursuing these targets as they see best, local actors provide the information necessary for regulators to revise their standards and goals and receive information on the performance of others that guides further experimentation. Thus the new framework forces continuous improvements in both regulatory rules and environmental performance while heightening the accountability of the actors to each other and the larger public.

The rolling-rule regime should not be confused with voluntarism, if that term is understood to imply the abdication of public authority and responsibility to private actors, singly or in groups. Nor is it merely devolution of authority from the federal government to smaller units. For while the rolling-rule regime radically expands the bounds of local autonomy and demands deep participation by private as well as public actors, it also requires accountability. Central authorities ensure that local units live up to their commitments by coordinating their activities, monitoring their performance, pooling their experiences, and enforcing feasible standards that emerge from their practice. But unlike conventional, hierarchical forms, in which subordinate parts answer to the center's authoritative command, rolling-rule regulation creates a collaborative and mutual accountability of center to parts, parts to center, parts to other parts, all to the whole enterprise—and to the public generally.

This reorientation is little noticed because of the sheer improbability of its success, given current assumptions about interest-group politics and failed public institutions. Environmentalists are taken to be inveterate opponents of industrialists or real estate developers, just as officials of federal, state, and local government are taken to be natural adversaries. How can all of these cooperate continuously for the long term under rapidly shifting conditions and even more rapidly evolving knowledge of the world?

We will argue that this emergent regulatory regime owes its success precisely to a counterintuitive but durable form of practical deliberation between and among environmentalists, developers, farmers, industrialists, and officials from distinct, perhaps competing, subdivisions of government: parties who are conventionally thought to be antagonists. In this problem-solving process, disciplined consideration of alternative policies leads protagonists to discover unanticipated solutions provisionally acceptable to all. Further deliberation leads to successive redefinitions of self-interest that permit robust collaborative exploration, including revision of institutional boundaries, procedures, and even ideas of what is feasible. In avoiding the notorious inflexibility of centralized command systems and the problems of information gathering associated with market-based mechanisms, the rolling-rule regime achieves levels of cooperation and environmental performance beyond the reach of either. At the limit, the practical successes of this form of deliberation in solving problems suggest the possibility of a directly deliberative form of participatory democracy in environmental regulation—and elsewhere as well.

A New Architecture

We start where many of these reforms began: with the frustration of environmental activists, managers of regulated firms, ordinary citizens, and regulators with the shortcomings of centralized command regulation on one hand and at the impracticality of market-based correctives on the other.

Command and Market

The distinguishing feature of centralized regulation is its claim to a modest omniscience. Though regulators renounce the pretension to complete knowledge of a complex and changing world, they nonetheless attempt to determine enduring solutions to well-specified problems. The result of this combination of confidence and self-deprecation is regulation that, piece by piece, attempts too little and too much.

There is too little regulation in the world of centralized command because detailed regulation requires sharp boundaries between what is regulated, and what is not (otherwise, rule making would require plain old, immodest omniscience). But under complex and changing conditions, problems just outside the regulated zone will frequently turn out to be just as significant as those within it. For example, the Endangered Species Act applies only to species nearing extinction. And it is immeasurably harder to save a species once it is sufficiently imperiled to qualify than when it is merely in decline. Similarly, the Clean Water Act (CWA) regulates gross and concentrated emissions of a handful of pollutants by large and conspicuous polluters such as factories and waste treatment facilities. The more varied and diffuse effluents of households and farms, though less obvious and harder to measure, may cause greater damage overall, but remain essentially unregulated.

But where it does aim for more definitive solutions, centralized command often regulates too much. The best available solution at the moment of adoption may have long-term, unintended consequences that outweigh early gains. Or the very successes of the best current solution may hinder the search for better ones. Even when the parties to the original rule suspect that they have been overtaken by events, fear of reopening discussions may prevent them from taking advantage of new opportunities. Those who broadly speaking favor regulation worry that confessing error opens the door to backsliding and jeopardizes their authoritative claims. Those who generally oppose regulation worry that new rules may expose them to even greater costs than the old. For example, some rules prescribe the use of specific "best" technologies to trap pollutants before they are introduced into the air or water—despite the possibility of improvements in these technologies, or the possibility that others could prevent the production of pollutants in the first place.

The 1980s brought two kinds of market-simulation proposals that promised to correct these defects. One focused on trades among polluting units. The other, cost-benefit analysis, focused on methods for analyzing the trade-offs implicit in competing regulatory proposals. Both approaches recognize that effective centralized regulation requires more knowledge than it can summon, and therefore would leave crucial choices to decentralized actors. But neither approach delivered on its promises of orderly decentralization.

To see why, consider the first and most familiar of these two proposals: to create "tradable emissions permits" that allow firms to pollute specified quantities of specified substances. In such a system, a central regulator identifies the regulated substance and establishes an overall cap on emissions based on the harm it causes and an estimate of reasonably attainable reductions. The regulator then assigns initial permit allotments to current polluters, creates trading rules and a compliance-monitoring regime, and lets the magic of the market do the rest. Polluters facing low costs of abatement will reduce their emissions and sell their excess permits at a profit to higher-cost abaters, who find it more economical to purchase permits than to make reductions themselves. As trades continue, the costs of abating a unit of pollution will stabilize around a market price. Thus every dollar spent to protect the environment from the regulated substance will ultimately buy as much protection as every other dollar, and society will achieve a goal of which the social planner can only dream: efficient allocation of the resources spent on pollution reduction.

Despite their modest claims to knowledge, market-simulating mechanisms ultimately share with centralized command regulation a demand for information they cannot satisfy. All markets—including those in pollution permits, water rights, and land—require extraordinary quantities and varieties of information. Among these are precise definitions and allocations of ownership rights, costs, and other terms for their transfer, as well procedures for resetting prices or redistributing rights when initial allocations prove too generous, or too niggardly. Ordinary markets work because most of this information is amassed from decentralized actors. In artificial markets, created from the center, the information must first be accumulated (or specified) by the regulator. Before issuing permits that create these commodities, regulators must know how much of the pollutant is being emitted in the aggregate and by individual sources, how much environmental harm results from various levels of emissions, and what reductions are feasible. Moreover, because markets depend on secure ownership rights, there are limits on post hoc program corrections and thus excessive expectations of inhuman foresight from all-too-human regulators.

Nor is simple deregulation a viable alternative to centralized command or market simulation. The wave of environmentalism that produced the EPA and Clean Air and Clean Water Acts has evolved into a robust popular movement that insists on public supervision of environmental hazards. Environmentalism, as a commitment to public stewardship of the biosphere, is now a securely established political fact. The only live debate is about the appropriate level of environmental protection, and how best to achieve it.

Novelty?

This abiding commitment to environmental protection has begun to weave bits of the old programs and a few innovations into a novel regulatory framework. This framework discounts the possibility of central, panoramic knowledge more steeply than either centralized command or market-simulating regulation, and it puts a higher premium on collaborative processes that allow central and local actors to learn from one another and from their actions in the world. It would use these surprises to revise the rules that frame collaboration, then seek further discoveries under guidance of the more capable frame, and so on. The philosophy of this architecture is pragmatist: while it rejects immutable principles, it keeps faith with the idea that we can always institutionalize better ways of learning from the inevitable surprises that experience offers us.

The new framework embraces local autonomy and broad accountability. Local actors—firms, local governments, local representatives of federal agencies, or representatives of all these acting together in composite entities—are given the responsibility, subject to general guidelines, to devise suitable measures within a broad policy area, say, the management of a watershed or habitat, or the reduction of toxics. Moreover, they devise measures by which they will assess their progress toward the goals they have set and mechanisms for correcting practice in light of actual performance.

In return for this autonomy, local actors agree to pool information on their performance, plans, and metrics—on how they are doing, how they plan to improve, and what standards they use to assess performance—typically by reporting them to a central monitor. The central monitor uses these data, in consultation with local actors, to determine minimally acceptable levels of performance, plausible targets for improvement, generally acceptable methods for assessment, as well as acceptable and preferable methods of organizing participation in subsequent discussion of goals and measures. Interim standards and general measures become benchmarks. Referring to these, local units then reassess their own performance. Local criticism and national scrutiny discipline laggards. Local actors are accountable to one another, within any one locality, and to the nation as a whole. National institutions are exposed to the informed gaze of the collectivity of localities. The next round of experimentation takes account of the feedback from these results, and leads, through further comparisons, to revisions in the standards and measures, as well as national and local procedures. Because the emphasis throughout is on measurement, evaluation, and continuous improvement of performance, we will call this new architecture performance-based.

The performance-based framework emphasizes the continuing importance of local knowledge, and thus requires broader and deeper local participation in environmental regulation than earlier regimes contemplated as necessary. Indeed, it assumes that its predecessors failed in part because they ignored the knowledge diffused among the broader public. Its own success will therefore depend on organizing participation that systematically taps this information even as it places additional demands and confers new powers on citizens. Already, as we will see, work teams within firms are beginning to engage in pollution-reduction efforts directly linked to the reorganization of production. Similarly, as a result of growing attention to nonpoint-source pollution, small farms and households whose runoff influences conditions in local tributaries are being asked to engage in (and authorized to implement) the kind of self-assessment and pollution-reduction planning once presumed to be within the reach of only large firms.

But this broader participation must also be deeper than traditional forms. Voting, comment in public hearings, or advocacy in environmental movements—the familiar varieties of direct participation—are occasions for making citizens' voices count in public decision making. In a performance-based regime, the citizen is called on not merely to express an opinion, or demand a solution, but to help formulate and implement solutions. The idea is to exercise joint responsibility, not simply to defend group interests. In this process, the new institutions may transform the identities of the users themselves. To underscore these transformative possibilities we will speak of deep use and deep users to distinguish participation and participants in the new regime from those in the old.

So the pragmatist architecture promises regulation that is more effective than are the current arrangements, and more democratic—which sounds too good to be true. To see just how much truth there is in this promise, let's consider how things work in practice.

PERFORMANCE-BASED REGULATION

A diverse set of recent innovations in environmental regulation shows how crucial components of this architecture are feasible in a wide array of settings, even if none of these settings contains all the relevant elements. On one side, this incompleteness is a vulnerability: each of these programs must eventually address its unanswered questions. On the other side, the fact that these experiments have been able to substitute novel components for the traditional ones in piecemeal fashion displays the adaptability of the overall architecture. It is hard to imagine that these programs could ever be built if each of its key components depended simultaneously upon the implementation of all the others.

For convenience we will group the cases by policy area. Thus the Toxics Release Inventory (TRI), the Massachusetts Toxics Use Reduction Act (TURA) of 1989, and Responsible Care control industrial pollutants while the Chesapeake Bay Program and HCPs aim to regulate watersheds and other ecosystems.

Information Matters

The Toxics Release Inventory is a federal right-to-know measure that forces some thirty thousand facilities to publicly report their releases of toxic chemicals. Enacted in response to the catastrophic 1984 explosion of a Union Carbide facility in Bhopal, India, its roots lie in a broad domestic movement against environmental hazards. That movement dates to the Love Canal scandal of 1978, when large amounts of toxic industrial chemicals were found to have been buried on a site where a local elementary school was later built. The resulting anger and activism connected the battle for information—what chemicals were present in what quantities, and what the health risks were—to defense of home, family, and neighborhood, and set the tone for a new style of local, lunch-pail environmentalism. Hundreds of communities organized to demand cleanups of toxic waste disposal sites, and to receive information under the banner of the community's right-to-know. That movement represented an extension of earlier efforts focused on the workplace, where activists had been seeking the right-to-know about job-related toxic exposures since the early 1970s. By the mid-1980s, locally based movements had already won right-to-know laws in at least thirty states and sixty-five cities and counties. Popular participation created a political atmosphere in which Congress, faced with the fears crystallized by Bhopal, reacted swiftly, and with little regard for the niceties of conventional administration.

The TRI requires that private and government-run facilities meeting statutory size requirements report only estimates of the amounts of some 650 chemicals transferred off-site, or routinely or accidentally released. Since passage of the Pollution Prevention Act (PPA) of 1990, facilities also must report transfers of listed chemicals within the plant and efforts at pollution reduction and recycling. The data are publicly available in print and on the Internet in both raw form and as tables comparing amounts released by substance, facility, industry, and location. Though failure to file a required report may result in penalties, inaccurate reporting does not. While the EPA does little to verify the accuracy of emissions reports, citizens may sue firms for failure to comply with the TRI's disclosure provisions. Data they obtain can then be used to establish violations of other, substantive statutory obligations, or as a lever by which to apply public pressure for improvements.

From the standpoint of the traditional regulatory regime, the TRI is an environmental "regulation," in the minimal sense of formally requiring disclosure of a body of information from which environmental rules and standards, fixed or rolling, might eventually be fashioned or enforced. Its operation therefore constitutes a rough test, under admittedly favorable circumstances, of whether benchmarking in general—and benchmarking of "alarming" information in particular—can play the central role that we have attributed to it in synchronizing performance-improving efforts.

The effects of the TRI strongly suggest that it can. First, the collection and publication of TRI data immediately disciplines polluting private actors. Public comparisons of polluters compiled by journalists or community activists from TRI data also lead to significant declines in the share value of publicly traded firms that show poorly. These reputational and financial market penalties give managers strong incentives to either reduce their toxics emissions or shade their reporting estimates to appear cleaner than they are.

As the EPA itself has noted, in making possible comparisons across regions and facilities, the release of information about toxics has allowed federal, state, and local governments to cooperate with the public and industry to "evaluate existing environmental programs, establish regulatory priorities, and track pollution control and waste reduction progress." In particular, states such as Massachusetts, Oregon, New Jersey, Washington, and Minnesota are using this collaborative redirection of regulatory activity to refine reports on the use of toxics and improve the pooling of the resulting information. Of these more-developed pooling programs, the most established, comprehensive, and influential was created by the TURA, Massachusetts' Toxics Use Reduction Act.

The TURA both broadens and extends the TRI. It broadens by requiring firms to report not only toxic releases, but also use or generation of toxics in any stage of production. The TURA further requires that these reports be connected to biannual toxics use reduction plans. Sometimes these plans are formulated by managers or process engineers alone, but frequently they are produced by problem-solving teams that include production workers as well. On the basis of such benchmarking surveys of possibilities, firms specify in the plan particular measures to be adopted, the schedule for implementing them, and two- and five-year reduction targets. Although the TURA established the general goal of reducing use of toxics in Massachusetts by 50 percent by 1997, and penalizes "willful" violations of the reporting and planning requirements, the act sets no more specific performance standards, nor does it penalize failure to act on reduction plans. Thus, rather than fix objectives and compel their attainment, the TURA furthers the TRI strategy of using the obligation for self-monitoring to induce firms and citizens to acquire information that reveals problems and helps formulate their solution.

At the same time, the TURA extends and helps formalize industry efforts at improved environmental performance both by creating a peer inspectorate to review the usage reduction plans and by providing technical consulting services. The TURA requires that plans be certified by toxics use reduction planners. Planner certification in turn requires individuals to complete various training programs and classes. The act accordingly established a Toxics Use Reduction Institute (TURI) at the Lowell campus of the University of Massachusetts to develop the curricula and provide these courses, inform industry or the public of developments in this area, and conduct research necessary to these activities. It also established the Office of Technical Assistance to assist firms (particularly small, first-time filers) in meeting their TURA obligations, and to help coordinate the provision of relevant services by the public and private sectors. Taken together, plans, planners, TURI, and the Office of Technical Assistance create an inspection system in which current conditions in individual firms or industrial segments can be compared with one another and with academic understanding of best practices, even as that understanding improves through exposure to innovative firms. Finally, the TURA provides a high-level governance structure that periodically suggests modifications of the new state services and reporting requirements in the light of its evaluation of progress towards the act's original reduction target.

This apparatus seems to work. From 1990 to 1995, the production-adjusted use of toxic chemicals fell by 20 percent in Massachusetts and the generation of toxic by-products by 30 percent. Furthermore, the toxics use planning requirement has enabled firms to discover significant net benefits of pollution prevention and increase their support for the public institutions that facilitate this process. Nor were these benefits offset for the firms by the costs of preparing reports and plans; 86 percent of all respondents said they would continue to plan even absent legal requirements.

The Need for a Public Role

Responsible Care is a Chemical Manufacturers' Association (CMA) program to reduce pollution through disciplined error detection and elimination by its member firms. The program, which started in 1988, effectively accepts the key assumptions of the rolling-rule regulatory regime. This is a vast undertaking: the CMA's roughly two hundred members account for about 95 percent of domestic production of basic chemicals, and the chemical sector as a whole accounts for half of the six billion pounds of toxics generated each year in the United States. But the CMA attempts to implement these mechanisms solely through private parties, with no government coordination and no public use of the relevant data. The core of Responsible Care consists of six "disciplines" that oblige firms to link pollution prevention efforts to their production processes. The program sets target dates for installing the new disciplines, advises member firms to monitor progress toward their goals, and helps document and disseminate best practices.

The results of Responsible Care are so far inconclusive, and the reason is close at hand in the configuration of the CMA. On the one side, as a trade association, the CMA depends on a consensus of its members for the authority to act. On the other, the sincere implementation of Responsible Care requires it to act as regulatory authority that can sanction members who do not discipline themselves. Whenever these sanctions threaten members' separate interests to the point of menacing consensus, the CMA vacillates, and Responsible Care risks degenerating into a public relations maneuver.

The new architecture we have outlined suggests that greater transparency and public accountability can overcome this stalemate. We find supportive evidence in the evolution of earlier, strikingly similar efforts at private regulation in the nuclear power–generating industry housed in the Institute of Nuclear Power Operations (INPO). These efforts succeeded only when the system of self-monitoring was placed under the aegis of public institutions and authority. Like Responsible Care, INPO grew out of a public relations crisis: it was formed in 1979, nine months after the Three Mile Island disaster. Like Responsible Care, INPO was designed as a private effort and was financed by the utilities.

From the outset INPO's chief activities consisted of pooling the industry's operating experience, establishing benchmarks to distill the lessons there, and then evaluating individual power plants according to their ability to meet those benchmarks. Operating information is gathered initially through the Significant Event Evaluation Information Network. INPO officials sift event reports to distinguish harmless disruptions of operations from dangerous ones. They then circulate analyses of the causes of the dangerous disruptions and ways to prevent them in significant operating experience reports. Industry operating experience reviews are then conducted periodically to assess the ability of particular plants to make effective use of the information provided by the reports.

This collection and dissemination of information to the immediate actors did not produce large improvements in performance. By the mid-1980s, it became clear that the effectiveness of INPO as a new center for performance improvement through information pooling depended crucially on its ability to divulge what it learned about the industry and individual firms to broader circles of participants. These would have to include high-level managers, boards of directors, and ultimately the Nuclear Regulatory Commission (NRC).

The broader diffusion began in late 1984, when INPO began to rank plants and make the results available to the CEO of the utility operating the power plant, the utility's board of directors, and the responsible public service commissions and the NRC. The NRC, in effect, retains the formal authority to promulgate regulations, but it either adopts the standards in training, maintenance, and other matters elaborated by INPO or simply acknowledges best practices defined by the institute without formalizing them. In addition to peer discipline and the authority derived from close cooperation with the NRC, INPO can suspend uncooperative member utilities. Thus, although there are no civil or criminal penalties for noncompliance with INPO standards, the institute found means to resolve the problems that now plague Responsible Care and thereby achieve notable safety improvements.[2]

Diffuse Problems

The Chesapeake Bay Program, which grew up alongside the EPA and is responsible for protecting and restoring the largest estuarine system in the United States, is at once the most extensive, mature, institutionally complex, and successful of the ecosystem regimes emerging in the new regulatory framework. Though the Clean Water Act regulated point-source polluters of the bay such as factories and power plants, it did not regulate pollution, more threatening to the bay, that derived from nonpoint sources such as farms, construction sites, lawns, landfills, septic tanks, and city streets. The program's exemplary accomplishment has been to address this more diffuse problem amid radically changing ideas of the exact nature of the threat, and how, ecologically and institutionally, to respond to it. Such is the attractive power of its example that the EPA is currently trying to model its new programs on the Chesapeake Bay Program, with the apparent intent of eventually reconfiguring regulation under the CWA itself.

The Chesapeake Bay Program emerged from a broad citizen movement, concerned with the degradation of a beautiful but fragile ecosystem that to this day evokes widespread pride and vigilance from residents, farmers, and businesspeople alike. In 1966—four years before the first Earth Day and six years before the passage of the CWA—these citizens formed the Chesapeake Bay Foundation as an advocacy organization to "Save the Bay." At the behest of this group, among others, congressional leaders funded a major six-year EPA study in 1973 to determine the status and causes of decline of the ecosystem. The report revealed a complex web of interrelated causes and alarming symptoms—such as declining fish and shellfish stocks—that spanned several states in the bay region.

In response to this report and continuing investigations, a multistate, interagency Chesapeake Bay agreement was signed in 1983 "to improve and protect water quality and living resources in the Chesapeake Bay ecosystem." The agreement—whose signatories included the EPA, the governors of Maryland, Virginia, and Pennsylvania, and the mayor of the District of Columbia—established the core institutional framework for future cooperative efforts. It created an executive council and an implementation committee to develop ecosystem restoration plans in conjunction with state and federal environmental agencies.

A second Chesapeake Bay agreement, signed in 1987, marked the next evolutionary phase of the program. Much more concrete than previous efforts, this accord established a regime of biological monitoring as the bedrock of future management efforts. It identified the "productivity, diversity, and abundance" of the bay's living resources as "the best ultimate measures of the Chesapeake Bay's condition," and set ambitious performance targets, including reduction of nutrient loadings by 40 percent by the year 2000. When further studies revealed that loadings in various tributaries had differential impacts on water quality in the bay itself, parties revised their systemwide goals and codified them in a 1992 commitment to develop tributary-specific nutrient reduction targets, strategies, and implementation tools. The 1992 amendments also established a specific, quantifiable biological monitoring regime, and executive council directives have added progressively more detailed commitments in such areas as a basinwide toxic reduction strategy, habitat restoration, wetlands protection, and agricultural nonpoint-source reduction.

All these arrangements and rearrangements are, however, the public face of deeper, less visible changes in the under-standing of environmental regulation that have come to shape the strategic reflections of the program's leading pro-tagonists. First, there is the realization that the more we learn about the ecology of the bay, the more surprising new findings will be. The second and third cumulative changes in the program's self-understanding are procedural. One concerns governance. The various agreements and the enti-ties that they establish constitute an institutional chassis for forming and re-forming governance mechanisms as chang-ing conditions warrant. In practice, the Chesapeake Bay Program has employed a grab bag of regulatory techniques, legal instruments, and voluntary measures. Above all, it has experimented with legal forms. Many of its policies build concerted packages from disparate administrative and legis-lative measures in typically segregated arenas such as "land use," "air pollution," "water pollution," "public lands man-agement," "fisheries management," and "wildlife conserva-tion." More specifically, many actions of the Chesapeake ex-ecutive council advancing such packets take the form of "directives." These are joint executive decrees of dubious le-gal pedigree and status. Yet they are regarded as, at a mini-mum, morally binding commitments on the part of each executive to use all available powers and authorities to carry out the stated commitments.

These arrangements work well enough for adjusting program activities within broadly agreed-upon boundaries. But more traditional forces come into play in larger redefinitions of purpose. In such moments, the very fluidity of the internal governance of the program becomes a liability, as external interlocutors seek, in vain, to determine the authoritative voice of an institutional ensemble that adjusts precisely by not having one.

The other change concerns citizen participation. Through the 1960s and early 1970s, participation in the program meant conventional public education through publications, public meetings, hearings, and mass media. When it became clear that the level of monitoring required to manage the bay and its tributaries was beyond the technical and financial capacity of government alone, emphasis shifted to more active, deeper forms of participation—essentially, teaching large numbers of volunteers to mimic the monitoring and reporting protocols developed by scientific experts, to produce a larger volume of reasonably reliable monitoring data. In the process, ordinary citizens would become quasi-experts by imitation. In the 1980s, the program explicitly equated participation with the emulation of expert knowledge.

The recent emergence of a "tributary strategy" emphasizing the need for stream-specific goals and implementation measures, marks the third reconceptualization of citizens' roles and their relationship to experts. Continuing surprises to expert judgment have led, reasonably enough, to the conclusion that the required level of specificity in planning and implementation is now beyond the capacity of experts alone. Nor can the necessary measures be developed by the lay public simply by following precise routines or protocols defined by the experts. Instead, responsibility is devolved to semiautonomous "tributary teams" made up of government officials, scientific experts, agricultural and industry representatives, and citizen volunteers. As a group they become experts with regard to their own tributaries, drawing on a unique mix of local knowledge, expert science (adapted to local needs), and basinwide experience to become the authors and implementers of the tributary strategy. Because measures can be tailored to the local circumstances of each watershed part, the tributary teams are simultaneously more effective and equitable in the burdens they impose than are the uniform statewide measures. Together, these changes lend plausibility to the idea of broad, continuing, and deeply informed citizen participation in environmental affairs that, unlike the first wave of backyard environmentalism, constructs as much as it obstructs.

Putting the Pieces Together

Among the most dynamic and supple prototypes of the new regulatory architecture is the HCP, which ironically emerged out of one of the most rigid of all environmental

laws: the Endangered Species Act. Section 9 of the act pro-
hibits the "taking" of listed wildlife species. "Take" includes
both direct injury and habitat modification that "kills or
injures wildlife by significantly impairing essential behavior patterns, including breeding, feeding or sheltering."[3] In
application, this simple language becomes a sweeping, in-
flexible rule with the potential to bar a broad range of land
development and resource extraction activities wherever
endangered species have been identified. Not surprisingly,
landowners, industries, and communities complain that
they are unfairly singled out under a harsh and arbitrary rule
that provides dubious species protection benefits.

In 1982, Congress responded by authorizing the issuance
of permits to "take" listed species if the taking is "incidental
to, and not the purpose of" an otherwise lawful activity. To
secure a permit, the applicant must produce an HCP and
demonstrate that the taking will not appreciably reduce the
likelihood of the species' survival and recovery. The U.S.
Fish and Wildlife Service retains broad discretionary authority to add any terms and conditions it deems necessary
to ensure species survival. By April 1999, 254 plans, regulating more than eleven million acres, had been approved and
two hundred more were in various stages of development.[4]

Bruce Babbitt, appointed Secretary of the Interior in
1993, and his staff favored the HCP process. They saw it as
an opportunity to bring landowners and environmentalists
together to hammer out habitat conservation plans that
might provide greater ecosystem protection than strict ap-

plication of Section 9—without halting development and economic growth. To demonstrate the workability of this approach to the public, regulated communities, and even to their own field agents, Babbitt and his associates would have to intervene in local HCP processes to elaborate a real and attractive alternative to traditional ESA enforcement.

Opportunities to do just this arose in San Diego and Orange Counties, where urban sprawl had already replaced much of the coastal sage scrub ecosystem with tract housing, shopping malls, and office parks. This, in turn, had shrunk and badly fragmented the habitat of local species like the California gnatcatcher, a songbird native to the Southern California coastal region. Yet when the gnatcatcher was proposed for listing under the ESA's Section 9's prohibition against "taking," that threatened to bring lucrative development in fast-growing San Diego and Orange Counties to an abrupt halt.

Compared to the listing, almost any alternative seemed reasonable to landowners, developers, and state and local government officials. The ESA allowed them to use the HCP process as a framework for negotiation. A California statute, the Natural Communities Conservation Planning Act, linked motive to framework by providing for a process (initially voluntary) that brought together landowners, state and local officials, conservationists, and other interested parties to develop integrated, regional-level ecosystem protection plans. They negotiated the first of a new generation of participatory and performance-based landscape-scale, multispecies HCPs in San Diego, Orange, and Riverside Counties.

Jointly formulated by developers, public officials, conservationists, and scientists, these plans require landowners to dedicate large tracts of land for exclusive use as habitat reserves for unlisted as well as listed species. They restrict development in buffer zones adjacent to the reserves to provide additional habitat benefits. Biological and environmental monitoring regimes, governance institutions, and funding mechanisms are put in place, and a range of "adaptive management" measures are specified, allowing adjustments to be made and contingency plans to kick in, based on the results of monitoring, new scientific information, and changes in conditions. In return, landowners are awarded "incidental take" permits that allow them to develop their remaining lands in accordance with the overall plan. The agreements are controversial among environmentalists,[5] some of whom prefer strict application of Section 9, and among landowners and developers, some of whom see the HCP process as legalized extortion. But many leading environmentalists, landowners, public officials, and scientists contend that, on the whole, these agreements produce more, better, and more sophisticated ecosystem management regimes than would emerge from even the strictest application of Section 9.

The inclusiveness and sophistication of these Southern California HCPs illuminate the promise of the new regulatory regime and offer a scalable example for the almost five hundred plans that are in development or have already been approved. While many of these are quite limited in scope, others are far more ambitious in their measures and goals and innovative in their internal architecture. Increasingly, HCPs are formulated by diverse affected parties and move beyond basic land use planning approaches to embrace water quality and stream flow measures, ecosystem restoration projects, forestry and agricultural "best management practices," and a variety of other implementation measures.[6]

But these Southern California successes are slow to diffuse to all HCPs because the emergent nationwide conservation planning regime is by and large unable to pool the information generated by local projects or to systematically learn from innovative developments, trends, successes, and errors. Such pooling as does occur is done mainly by the U.S. Fish and Wildlife Service,[7] whose highly decentralized internal structure has so far proved far better at dispersing authority to local decision makers than at reviewing the ensuing decisions. The result is nearly unsupervised local autonomy with correspondingly wide variations in the performance of HCPs from one place to another. Thus local circumstance, seldom corrected by national discipline, determines whether an HCP monitors its progress well or poorly,[8] or whether its decision making is accessible not only to local deal makers, but also to independent scientists, conservationists, and generally informed citizens. Often, in fact, HCPs amount to an agreement between a permit seeker and a service field agent. Where the experience of the Chesapeake tributary teams shows that open participation and good science may be mutually reinforcing, this kind of involution—especially in the absence of rigorous monitoring—can lead to self-deluding celebrations of expert powers and so to underestimation of the combined political, scientific, and practical complexity of large-scale ecosystem management.[9] At the worst, it can undermine the democratic legitimacy of HCPs by transforming them into unprincipled backroom deals between regulators and the regulated.[10]

In response to such concerns two measures—a new U.S. Fish and Wildlife Service guidance and the Endangered Species Recovery Act of 1999 (H.R. 960, or the Miller bill)—have been proposed to create a minimal informational infrastructure for the coordination of the HCPs, and thereby to improve performance of individual plans with respect to monitoring and accessibility. As concerns monitoring, the guidance directs the service to create a database that tracks basic plan features such as permit duration, acreage covered, species and habitat details, authorized take, and permitted activity. It may also record monitoring programs, actual take, operational adjustments, and field visit reports.[11] Similarly, the Miller bill directs bilateral monitoring of the implementation of HCPs and their biological outcomes; permit holders would be required to report publicly on actions taken in accordance with the plan, status of jeopardized species, and progress toward objective, measurable biological goals, and the secretary would be required to report on the implementation and quantitative biological progress of each plan every three years.

As concerns accessibility, the FWS guidance responds tepidly by extending the Administrative Procedure Act's after-the-fact "notice and comment" period from thirty to sixty days and offering the only slightly more ambitious proposal to add advisory and informational committees in cases of large-scale HCPs. The Miller bill goes further, instructing the department to take steps to ensure balanced public participation in the development of large-scale, multiple landowner, and multispecies plans. Without better institutionalizing the distinctive contributions that the public can make to ecosystem governance—information, monitoring capacity, oversight, and democratic legitimacy —reformers risk losing elements critical to a successful process. Optimistically considered, these measures, or something like them, will lay the groundwork for a TRI-style information-based pooling system whose own initial shortcomings will be incrementally corrected even as the emergent infrastructure makes it possible to begin overcoming, locale by locale, the defects of disjointed decentralized ecosystem management.

Weaving the Whole

Does this tale of environmental reorientation merit further elaboration, beyond recounting these illustrations? On one interpretation, the independent emergence of this architecture in diverse settings attests to its robustness across local environments and political regimes. Formulating a comprehensive regulatory design might then be unnecessary because some groups will eventually discover it, or unhelpful because it would shackle novel local experimentation to half-baked and half-replicable experiences.

This incremental view is too optimistic, and in any case has already been overtaken by events: federal agencies are extending and elaborating the emergent principles of innovation by undertaking large projects that aim to replicate the kinds of regulatory successes we have been examining. The piecemeal decentralization of authority from federal to subnational authorities has excited the interest of the states. And crucially, Congress is noticing the anomalies of the new regimes as viewed in the light of the legislation from which their authorization is derived.

Like it or not, debate about the legitimacy of the performance-based systems is about to be on the agenda. At the core of that debate will be a fundamental question: How can directly deliberative, problem-solving regimes coexist with the institutions of pluralist democracy? This question arises, we will now see, as much when the reformers aim for self-limiting modesty, as when they are more ambitiously expansive. Precisely because the problem is ubiquitous, consolidation of the new architecture will, we believe, in the end depend on an open validation—probably through Congress—of the changes that have emerged as much outside the current order as within.

For an illustration of the vulnerability of administrative reform not backed by law, consider the recent HCP experience. High officials in the Department of the Interior argued that under conditions of modern complexity, government can at most reveal the possibilities of new forms of collective problem solving through a discrete politics of the deed. Once working models of the alternative have proved their worth, the equilibrium mechanisms of pluralist society ensure that the incipient experiments develop in ways society judges fair and effective. With regard to the HCPs, for instance, local "underenforcement" that threatened vulnerable species would be registered by national environmental groups, who would press the authorities for corrective action; "overenforcement" would conversely provoke protests by local property owners and move their national representatives to corresponding interventions. Aggressive advocates of more comprehensive strategies misunderstand what government under modern conditions can do, and imperil what has been done by bringing it to the attention of busybodies.

This peculiar optimism seems misplaced. Why assume that the dueling political powers produce an exquisite balance, rather than a welter of clashing rules, or a self-canceling swing of policy from "too much" to "too little" protection of endangered species or prosecution of other goals? In recent decades, in policy area after policy area, this, not harmony, has been the outcome. The introduction of forms of direct deliberation at the local levels will, if anything, make pluralist interest balancing at the highest levels less practicable than before. Institutions such as HCPs work precisely by uncovering, through experimentalist investigation, potential solutions initially unknown even to the local actors. How, and on the basis of which incentives, will the pluralist rule makers at the center come to know of the local discoveries? If they know, what solutions will they in turn support? If higher-ups predictably rule in ignorance, indifference, or hostility to these innovations, why should local actors engage in experimentalist exploration at all?

The Miller bill could furnish an elegant resolution to this clash between directly deliberative and pluralist decision making in the case of HCPs. The proposed bill in effect carries forward the careful environmentalist criticism of the promise of HCPs. It aims to solve much of the problem simply by requiring the Department of the Interior to respect minimum HCP conditions. Thus, to be recognized as valid, the HCPs must incorporate objective, measurable biological goals aimed at species recovery, a regime to monitor the biological status of each covered species, regularized reporting, and appropriate adaptive management measures. Development of large-scale HCPs involving multiple landowners or multiple species would require substantial public participation, and to ensure consistency, transparency, and accountability within individual HCPs and throughout the system as a whole, the secretary would be required to review each HCP triennially and recommend such adjustments as are necessary to ensure species recovery, and publish an annual report on the status of all HCPs.

Thus Congress, if it passes the Miller bill, would subtly modify both its own legislative role and that of the administrative agency. Congress's role would shift from the familiar one of setting some relatively circumscribed public goal—protecting endangered species—and delegating responsibility for achieving it to a federal rule maker, to authorizing and conferring pluralist political legitimacy on the constitutive framework under which citizens as local agents can experimentally determine how to pursue a presumptively broad and changing project: protecting and restoring habitats. The role of the Department of the Interior would shift from relying on its own expertise and judgment to help craft the agreements and determine their acceptability, to rigorously policing a framework within which a broad and open circle of participants, local and national, can determine for themselves whether particular HCPs, and the institution taken as a whole, are meeting the goals it sets for itself. Familiar fights will of course continue, but the rules for adjudicating them will change.

None of this is likely to happen immediately. But the very variety of ways in which deep users are prospectively combining the current, imperfect buildings blocks suggests that there will also be many opportunities to crystallize this democratic regulatory reorientation in political discussion, and so to insert a promising new item on the reform agenda.

DEMOCRATIC REFORM

The great dilemma for twentieth-century democrats has been the conflict between efficiency and the values of fairness and self-determination served when citizens rule themselves. The mainstream view is simply that markets are the most efficient instruments for allocating resources and hence that any democratically inspired adjustments to market operations or redirection of their proceeds induces inefficiency. Even the great currents of American popular reform—such as Jacksonianism, populism, and progressivism, which shared a deep fear of the predatory power of economic elites—themselves treat private ordering as a kind of precious nature preserve, easily disrupted by excesses of democratic participation.

Jacksonians, populists, and their more recent descendants, Reagan-era monetarists and supply-siders, sought to reform finance once and for all. They aimed to remake the market so that the everyday transactions by which citizens effected their economic advancement would not result in accumulations of wealth and influence that might then be turned against their freedom. Through these movements runs the thread of the characteristically American distinction between well-ordered markets as the instrument and guarantee of legitimate self-assertion and perverted ones as the tool of domination.

The progressive impulse, in contrast, seeks redress not in a once-and-for-all institutional reform, but rather in an enduring and self-reinforcing shift of authority away from contending class interests and toward the trusteeship of a circle of technically versed experts. The hope—in the new century's struggle against trusts and corrupt political machines as well as in recent battles with cigarette makers, pharmaceutical companies, and drug dealers—is to attenuate the destructive contest between elite and mass by interposing stewards of the common good who would themselves be disciplined by rigorous inquiry.

The environmental reforms we have discussed arose within these channels but overflowed their original banks. They commingle these streams of reform and reveal in their novel course the most improbable of possibilities: that participation of a directly deliberative kind, far from being a charge against efficiency, may be today a precondition for it.

The profusion of participation that makes backyard environmentalism work springs from our traditional ideas of reform, yet holds promise of freeing us from deep limits to our idealism.

The inspiration of the TRI and, more diffusely, of the Chesapeake Bay Program, was the Jacksonian or populist notion that occulted powers were literally poisoning the people in pursuit of private gain. The remedy was to use government authority to force transparency, to require the disclosure to local communities of the additional information they needed to defend themselves from those who would poison them. Both had the distinctly Jacksonian flavor of efforts to reorder markets, not attack market order as such. Opponents of both programs disparage the ability of common people to digest and responsibly respond to the disclosures in terms that recall the nineteenth-century patrician fear and disdain of the tempestuous mob. Moreover, because both programs were launched with the intent of creating self-contained and self-enforcing mechanisms, neither anticipated the need, soon manifest, for higher-order mechanisms continuously to adjust the frame of intervention itself according to the findings of initial investigations.

The TURA, Responsible Care, and HCPs, in contrast, were progressive. All depend on the active participation of experts—toxics use reduction planners and conservation biologists—whose disciplining presence on both sides of the bargaining table is said to make the bargains possible and manageable once struck. The chief limitation of these programs has accordingly been the tension they create between the circle of experts, exchanging information openly among themselves, and the concentric circles of the more or less engaged public who are not formally included in the discussion but by virtue of their information and experience eventually move toward its center.

To establish these continuities between past and present is not, of course, to foretell a continuation of the old errors of Jacksonianism and progressivism. On the contrary, the confluence of expertise and market ordering of both traditions in the new regime holds the promise of transcending their separate limitations. Thus the successes of the TRI, as well as many aspects of the operation of certain HCPs or of INPO, shame the progressives in their deference to expertise and vindicate the Jacksonian faith in the capacity of citizens of govern their own affairs. Above all, the self-transformative successes of the Chesapeake Bay Program reveal the needless limitations of the Jacksonian faith in once-and-for-all solutions to problems of social order and vindicate the confidence of many progressives that the public could respond to its problems through institutionalized, deeply informed self-scrutiny in a way that John Dewey— the boldest of them all—could himself scarcely imagine. The common lesson is that expertise without local participation remains ignorant of crucial detail, and that localism unprovoked by expertise remains haplessly parochial.

* * *

To be sure, some parts of the established environmental movement continue to prefer the insider's game of pluralist grappling for influence at power centers. But other parts are reorganizing to take advantage of the local participatory possibilities of the emergent regime. For example, largely self-directed chapters of the Nature Conservancy and other, often ad hoc groupings of conservation-minded citizens are stepping forward on their own initiative to lead ambitious ecosystem-management projects, loosely coordinated by the flow of information to national conservation organizations and government agencies, and back again to other local projects. In these efforts, distinctions between the public sphere and the private begin to blur, as the citizen-authors of public policy come to view government at all levels as a partner to be recruited into a broadly collaborative effort, rather than as master rule maker or ultimate arbiter before whom they must come as supplicant or subject.[12]

Even at the pinnacle of the Washington environmental establishment, some see the need for self-redefinition and democratic renewal. The National Wildlife Federation, for one, candidly acknowledges that with habitat conservation programs now dominant in endangered species policy, decision-making authority has already shifted from the center to localities. Consequently, it says environmentalists' emphasis must also shift. No longer able to influence the substantive rules directly, the national organizations must instead work to ensure a deeply participatory local process, both by influencing the overall design of the regulatory architecture and by encouraging and supporting citizen participation in HCPs, locality by locality.[13] The national organizations thus begin to reinvent themselves as independent monitors of local performance and poolers of best practices, in effect becoming a separate and parallel repository for the rich flow of information generated by the new regime.[14] In this way, they position themselves simultaneously to monitor and offer informed critiques of the regime's design and performance overall and in the local particulars, and to provide local citizens an independent channel of information to guide, assist, and empower them in local efforts. Thus do participation, coordinated decentralization, and the open flow of information merge over time into a self-reinforcing system of deep use, and in so doing enrich our democratic polity.

Whatever the immediate outcomes of the struggles over environmental reform, backyard environmentalism has progressed far enough to make us insist on exploring the possibilities for augmenting and transforming our democracy before continuing to settle for less and less of it.

2

GOVERNMENT'S JOB

MATT WILSON AND ERIC WELTMAN

"Beyond Backyard Environmentalism" identifies and discusses some novel and important environmental policies and programs. Unfortunately, its thesis could be easily read to support government abdication of its fundamental responsibilities. It is the government's job to protect public health and the environment; it should not be the obligation of citizens to have to join "stream teams" or publicize the Toxics Release Inventory (TRI) data in order to enjoy clean water and air. Although citizen activism is at the core of our organization's mission, it is mostly successful in concert with government action, not in lieu of it.

In fact, citizens' engagement in environmental matters is the exception, not the rule, and is often made necessary when the government is not doing its job. Clean water and air should be a right enjoyed by everyone, not just those "squeaky wheels" with the time and assistance necessary to take up the battle for a safe environment.

In addition, Sabel, Fung, and Karkkainen overstate the significance of information, planning, and public involvement initiatives. In many circumstances, these initiatives may not be the best policy. When they do work, they do so in tandem with other policies, not by substituting for them.

{ 49 }

In fact, the TRI data and other public information is often used as a tool to prod government action to enforce permits and regulations, not to embarrass polluters into cleaning up their acts.

Different types of environmental threats necessitate different policies, making it unwise to endorse one model as the wave of the future. For example, "Beyond Backward Environmentalism" rightly praises the TURA as a model law for reducing industrial chemical use. For certain chemicals, however—where there is no safe threshold for exposure, or the toxin is persistent and builds up in the food chain—outright bans may be the safest and wisest policy. This was certainly the case for lead in gasoline, and may be equally so for perchloroethylene (perc), a dry cleaning solution, and MTBE, a gasoline additive.

In fact, the threat of the "stick" of bans, enforcement actions, and other stringent measures are necessary for the "carrot" of voluntary initiatives to work. For instance, Sabel, Fung, and Karkkainen state that "leading environmentalists, landowners, public officials, and scientists contend that, on the whole, [habitat conservation plans] produce more, better, and more sophisticated ecosystem management regimes" than strict application of the Endangered Species Act. Unfortunately, they cite no evidence to back this claim, nor do they even name any of the "leading environmentalists" who support it. More important, though, the threat of Endangered Species Act's Section 9 should be recognized as necessary to bring developers to the table for

the expedient compromises developed in habitat conservation plans. It is our experience that in negotiations with
companies over a cleanup plan, the power that citizens wield
is the threat of demanding government action; it is this
threat that brings companies to the table and ultimately
helps citizens have their demands met.

Again, Sabel, Fung, and Karkkainen tend to overstate
the success of their model initiatives, overlooking how they
work in tandem with other policies. For instance, they state
that the "publication of TRI data immediately disciplines
polluting private actors." They cite no evidence to substanti-
ate this, except for the anonymous claims of some "com-
mentators." We suspect, however, that the TRI data may
have had its greatest impact in embarrassing polluters in the
years when it was first released, and publicity was at its
height. When the latest data was released, to our knowledge, only one newspaper article highlighting a particular
polluter appeared in all of Massachusetts.

More important, the TRI data is a tool to encourage more
government action against polluters—not to embarrass
companies into conducting voluntary cleanups. For communities living with dirty air or polluted water, citizen activism is usually made necessary by a government willing to
overlook the problem as much as by the companies causing
the problem. This raises three key points. First, the TRI
data and other public information are not a substitute for
permit restrictions on pollution limits and other requirements; they are, in many situations, tools for citizens to en-

sure that the government fulfills its obligation to enforce these requirements. Second, the use of these strategies is necessary only in the unfortunate circumstances when the government is not doing its job.

Third, an extraordinary commitment of resources, skills, and time is required for information and public involvement opportunities to be effective in protecting public health and the environment. Many citizens—for example, single parents or families juggling several jobs—do not have the time to organize a campaign against a polluter, or participate in tributary protection planning. Moreover, most citizens lack the skills necessary to organize effectively against powerful corporations. In New England, the Toxics Action Center provides organizing strategies, media training, and legal tactics to residents who are fighting local environmental hazards. Yet not every state has a Toxics Action Center or a similar such organization. In addition, technical assistance is often necessary for citizens to understand the TRI data and the TURA information, and to determine what steps companies can take to clean up their acts. Yet, such assistance from the government is generally lacking; for these programs to truly fulfill their promise, grants should be made available for hiring consultants to advise grassroots groups.

The reality is that companies are more likely to have both the time and the expertise to participate in stream teams, habitat conservation plans, and the like. In fact, "Beyond Backyard Environmentalism" acknowledges that participation in habitat conservation plans varies from site to site, often including only a permit seeker and a government official, potentially "transforming them into unprincipled backroom deals between regulators and the regulated."

Which leads to the most important point: squeaky wheels should not get all the grease. Citizens' engagement in environmental matters is the exception, not the rule. Yet, it should not be only communities with residents willing and able to publicize the TRI data—and with newspapers willing to print them—that have clean air. "Stream teams" may be effective, but it should not be the obligation of citizens to form teams for every stream, lake, and river to ensure their cleanliness. These tools are often necessary for pressuring the government to fulfill its obligations to protect our health and safety. But the use of these tools by citizens should not be obligatory for living in a clean and safe environment.

AN APPEALING VISION

DANIEL J. FIORINO

Sabel, Fung, and Karkkainen offer a promising and, for the most part, astute vision of the future of environmental policy in this country. After nearly three decades of building an elaborate regulatory apparatus and further centralizing authority in Washington, policy makers are responding to demands for greater autonomy, flexibility, and participation. There are even signs that our adversarial approach to environmental regulation will eventually become more cooperative.

Many of us find this postbackyard environmentalism appealing. It is a world in which conflict is replaced by consensus. Citizens engage experts and administrators on vital issues. Regulatory agencies relax their technical-rationalist mode of operation in favor of a more populist orientation. Powerful national bureaucracies and activist organizations cede authority they have accumulated during the past thirty years, and allow local governments and citizens' groups more control over their environmental destinies. Traditional adversaries from industry, government, and environmental groups set aside years of distrust and work together for a better environment. And everyone engages in a kind of national learning seminar, in which goals are set, information on their achievement spreads throughout the policy system, multiple actors adapt their behavior in response to information, and goals are tightened as the capacity to meet them improves.

This is an appealing vision. And it is not the only such vision we have seen. The 1996 report of the President's Council for Sustainable Development made the case for a policy system that is more cooperative, participatory, collaborative, flexible, and decentralized. In two recent reports commissioned by Congress (in 1995 and 1997), the National Academy of Public Administration urged a shift toward a more performance-based, result-oriented policy system and urged that we create the flexibility, state-local authority, and citizen capacities needed to achieve it. And in an ambitious effort to build consensus among a range of influential stakeholders, the Enterprise for the Environment Initiative offered a vision of environmental policy making that was based on the same principles of participation, collaboration, and flexibility. Still, the policy response to each of these visions, and in many cases some fairly specific recommendations, has been less than resounding.

The greatest progress toward the kind of policy regime outlined by Sabel, Fung, and Karkkainen has been in regional or community-based environmental protection. The Chesapeake Bay Program experience is an excellent example. Many of the issues regarding nonpoint pollution, local land use, and economic growth were not addressed by national regulation, and there was ample room for the emergence of an adaptive, flexible, learning-based approach to the problem. In areas where regulation is more extensive, such as in industrial air, water, and waste pollution, the efforts to move toward a more flexible, responsive, performance-based approach have been far more difficult, as participants in Environmental Protection Agency's Common Sense Initiative and Project XL have found. In these efforts, a prescriptive legislative framework and traditionally adversarial relationships among parties, among other factors, presented barriers to the process of change.

Sabel, Fung, and Karkkainen attribute the growing interest in flexible, decentralized, participatory approaches to the rise of "backyard environmentalism." This activism was essentially reactive: citizens rose to protect their neighborhoods from threats (such as the siting of a waste treatment facility) or to demand attention to an existing threat (such as an abandoned industrial waste site). They argue that this movement laid a foundation for a new citizen activism, and with it demands for greater local autonomy and participation. But they give little attention to other factors that have contributed to the demands for change, such as the trend toward a "greening of industry" among leading firms, the change from a manufacturing-dominated economy to a services-dominated economy, and the growing impatience from nearly all quarters with a rigid, complex, and often inefficient regulatory system. What they call backyard environmentalism is part of the picture, but these other factors also drive the demands for change.

Some more specific points deserve comment. "Beyond Backyard Environmentalism" notes the limits of a command-and-control approach, in particular its demands on the knowledge held by regulators. For a top-down regulatory approach to work, regulators need lots of information about processes, costs, technologies, and other factors. They simply cannot be expected to stay current on all aspects of all sectors in today's dynamic, global economy. Although I agree that the benefits of marketable permits often are oversold, they do remove some of the information demands made on regulators by traditional regulation. Instead of government's making all of the decisions about process changes, investments in new technologies, and levels of production, each firm is allowed to make its own decisions within the context of the marketable permits trading-and-allocation system. A well-designed permit-trading program may serve as a building block of the decentralized, learning model of environmental policy making espoused in this article.

As to the Toxics Release Inventory (TRI), it has become known as one of the great unintended successes in the recent history of American public policy. It is seen as the stimulus for substantial reductions in pollution releases by a range of industrial firms who, sensitive to their public image and often surprised at what they did not know about their own releases, undertake to improve their performance in areas that are not required by existing regulation. While I agree that the TRI has been an impressive and innovative policy tool, I think we should keep it in perspective. First, the TRI might not have had the same effect had it not been for the backdrop of often stringent regulation. Some of the reductions may even have been in anticipation of future such regulation. Second, we do not know how widespread, deep, or lasting the effects of the TRI have been or will be. Firms react to bad news by acting to reduce emissions (or at least the larger, visible firms do). Before we stake the future of U.S. environmental policy on mandatory disclosure, however, I would want more information on the actual effects of the TRI.

The section on Responsible Care highlights an important and promising trend. Industry sectors are beginning to take collective responsibility for the effects of their activities on the environment. This trend is most pronounced in the chemical and nuclear power industries, where public scrutiny and potential for environmental catastrophe have stimulated industry self-regulation. But it is happening in other sectors as well, such as forest products and textile manufacturing. My own view is that these sector codes of environmental practice, issued by trade associations, offer a potentially powerful mechanism for improving environmental performance. They certainly deserve a role in the new kind

of environmental policy regime that Sabel, Fung, and Karkkainen lay out in their article. Their vision for the future
leaves several issues unaddressed. For example, what is the
role for technical expertise and bureaucratic authority in an
essentially democratic, populist policy regime? Is the public
willing to take on this expanded responsibility for determining environmental outcomes? If outcomes are based on
local priorities and negotiations, what is the role of national
standards? If national standards are not present, will local
citizens have the political clout to maintain high levels of
environmental performance? How will national regulatory
agencies and national environmental organizations (both of
which derive their power from federal legislation) be con-
vinced to turn over significant authority to local government and citizens groups? What we get here is a vision, but
little sense of how it might be translated into a new environmental policy regime.

These reservations aside, I heartily agree with their fundamental premise: the world is changing and environmental policy must change with it. Government no longer will
be able unilaterally to impose its will on powerful firms, especially those with a global reach. As the origins of backyard environmentalism show, the public will not defer
lightly to technical experts and administrative officials who
claim authority on what is in the public good. The pace of
change and complexity of modern manufacturing and the
rise of service industries, which have environmental conse-

quences as well, render traditional regulatory strategies obsolete. Just as economies and political systems modernize, so must institutions and capacities for solving and preventing environmental problems. The vision of a learning model of policy making that is participatory, flexible, adaptive, and decentralized is clearly the way to go. Now if we can just figure out how to get there.

GOOD COPS, BAD COPS

DEWITT JOHN

Sabel, Fung, and Karkkainen have a clear fix on the six-year-old debate about what others are calling "civic environmentalism" or "second-generation environmental policy." They describe this new form of governance accurately:

1. It engages diverse citizens, community leaders, polluters, and regulators in custom-designing environmental solutions for individual places and industries.

2. Regulators allow flexibility to businesses to redesign products, services, and production processes to minimize environmental impacts while still making a profit.

3. Regulators allow flexibility when the environmental results can be better. They, and the public, demand accountability, which requires vastly improved information about environmental conditions.

4. New technologies for monitoring environmental conditions will help provide such information; however, scientists must work as peers with citizens to collect data and interpret what it means.

This is the happy half of the story. The other half is that these new ways cannot replace strictly enforced national standards. We need both the "good cop" of government, willing to empower and support local problem-solving efforts, and the "bad cop" of government, standing ready to enforce national standards if necessary. Often the good cop is not persuasive if there is no bad cop waiting in the next room. The challenge is how to operate a tough regulatory regime alongside flexible civic deliberation.

Sabel, Fung, and Karkkainen might address more clearly three limits on civic environmentalism:

Borders: Many forms of air and water pollution cross borders. It is often difficult to get all interested parties around the negotiating table. Federal officials end up representing out-of-town and national interests. Recently thirty states negotiated a remarkable agreement about interstate movement of ozone. But in the end, they asked the EPA to incorporate the agreement into national regulations, and then some parties to the agreement promptly litigated the continuing points of disagreement.

Time: Collaborative problem solving is a demanding, often exhausting process. In most communities, citizens, local leaders, and businesses will keep talking only when there is a crisis and when there is a good chance of a mutually rewarding breakthrough. Often it is easier just to follow the prescriptive regulation because you can easily buy technology off the shelf to comply with the law. A multiyear study by the Natural Resources Defense Council (NRDC) and Dow Chemical recently uncovered dozens of ways to prevent pollution while also cutting costs. The returns on investment were excellent. But the dollars saved were so small that the company would not have bothered if NRDC had not helped out.

Money: Environmental issues have a consensual element: we all like clean air and water. But sometimes environmental politics are about real differences. Often businesses save millions by emitting a bit more pollution. So consensual problem solving works best when there is money to pay off the losers, for example, tax breaks for environmental equipment or purchases of conservation easements to protect species, watersheds, or open space. To make backyard or civic environmentalism work, the federal government must not only offer regulatory flexibility but also put up cash. The Chesapeake Bay Program, for example, is sustained partly by a powerful Maryland senator who sits on the EPA appropriations subcommittee.

The trend toward civic environmentalism is unstoppable. Citizens do demand answers that fit local conditions. New monitoring technologies help supply the information needed to measure performance and ensure accountability. Twenty moderate Republican and Democrat members of Congress recently offered "second-generation" legislative proposals, paralleling proposals in a 1997 report by the National Academy of Public Administration, which called the old EPA system "broken." Congress may be ready to invest billions of federal budget surpluses in protecting lands and water.

But there is a long way to go. Innovations like those that

Sabel, Fung, and Karkkainen celebrate are still "marginal," the academy reported. Statutes offer little encouragement to customized local problem solving. Engineers and lawyers skilled in drafting and defending detailed prescriptive regulations still dominate agencies. Indeed, since 1999 progress toward flexibility and has been slow—perhaps slowing.

The challenge to environmental agencies and to advocates of second-generation environmental governance is to explain how to fit the good cop and the bad cop into the same system. For example, flexibility includes devolution to states; states collect most data and they need different kinds of data than federal regulators need to ensure states do not abuse flexibility. So the EPA must simultaneously command and devolve. It is liberating to uncover a new way of addressing public concerns. The enthusiastic claims of Sabel, Fung, and Karkkainen have merit. Whatever its name, new forms of environmental governance will reinvigorate our republic and protect the environment more efficiently. But we must draw on multiple traditions. We can progress in a Jacksonian direction—though perhaps de Tocqueville is a better guide. And we need Madisonian pluralism too.

COMPENSATING CITIZENS

JACQUELINE SAVITZ

"Beyond Backyard Environmentalism" is more a wishful fantasy than a true analysis of any reorientation in environmental regulation. It portrays a world in which win-win situations abound, limited only by our willingness to build partnerships and work together through a participatory dialogue. Reality, unfortunately, is not that simple. In making the case that we are moving into this new paradigm, Sabel, Fung, and Karkkainen prematurely reject valuable regulatory programs, mischaracterize the programs used as examples, and misunderstand the motives of well-intentioned citizens whose families and livelihoods are threatened by "progress."

After centuries of human impacts on the American environment, it is premature to label three-decade-young "traditional regulations" a failure. The need for, much less the emergence of, the "new approach" described by Sabel, Fung, and Karkkainen to replace the current regulatory approach is not recognized by the majority of public-interest advocates. Participation by many organizations in these dialogues indicates a need for public involvement. But that does not mean that citizens no longer value more traditional approaches.

Conversely, corporate involvement in, and even initiation of, participatory programs likely does signify an interest in a new approach to regulation. The regulated community has spent billions of dollars to comply with environmental statutes, and millions more to undermine them. A new, nonregulatory approach could help achieve the primary goal of corporations: to minimize costs and maximize profits.

Most environmental advocates would agree that the effectiveness of an environmental program depends primarily on its achievement of environmental goals. Using Sabel, Fung, and Karkkainen's examples, one must ask: Did the TRI or TURA reduce toxic chemical use? Did the Chesapeake Bay Program increase the quality of the bay? These programs, among others, can be placed on a one to ten scale. Effective programs such as the Clean Water Act's water quality–permitting program are closest to ten; the TURA outranks the TRI somewhere in the mid-range; and the Chesapeake Bay Program and habitat conservation plans fall somewhere near the low end of the scale.

Through their initiation of public accountability, the TURA and TRI are credited with stimulating a reduction of toxic chemical use and release. A closer look at these programs, however, shows that they fail to illustrate large-scale reductions resulting from participatory dialogue. In actuality, each of these laws relies heavily on what Sabel, Fung, and Karkkainen refer to as "centralized command regulation." In addition to the fact that the TRI has mandatory reporting requirements, much of its perceived success has been attributed to coexisting regulations. For example, large reductions in the TRI releases, while indirectly stimulated by public awareness, came about due to mandatory phase-outs of chlorinated fluorocarbons. Other reductions touted as successes in the TRI are even less impressive paper reductions, resulting from changes in estimation procedures, or through chemical companies' successful attempts at chemical delisting.[1]

Most improvements in the Chesapeake Bay are attributable not to the Chesapeake Bay Program, but to the Clean Water Act permitting program, bans on phosphate detergents enacted by state governments in spite of staunch industry opposition, and sewage treatment plant upgrades.[2] None of these efforts boasts the type of participatory, nonregulatory process that Sabel, Fung, and Karkkainen espouse. Stripping citizens of a regulatory system inflicts a handicap that could lead only to negative consequences for the environment.

The concept of citizen involvement is actually more of a historical construct than a new development. As government evolved, citizens were appointed to serve as environmental stewards and, notably, were compensated for their time. Sabel, Fung, and Karkkainen do not envision compensating today's citizen stewards for the time and effort expended in the new system they describe; as a result, it confers what corporate lobbyists would call an unfunded mandate. Apparently, they envision a shift from citizens trained, compensated, and empowered to act as stewards to a decision-making citizenry that is disempowered, financially strapped, and as such at a severe disadvantage.

This is not fiction. Well-intentioned citizens of my parents' generation are often invited to the table without any resources to cover their travel or their time, and without support for outside technical assistance. They sit beside high-paid corporate lawyers and engineers and are expected to outargue the lawyers and outengineer the engineers. How could our parents be expected to provide better service to their neighbors in the absence of federal regulations that the federal government provides? Such citizen panels are more likely to serve as smoke screens than as effective advocates. Who better understands complex technical issues—your mother or the scientists paid by the public to protect it?

In this light, the "participatory approaches" touted in "Beyond Backyard Environmentalism" may instead be just another method for corporations to avoid regulations that were developed for the common good but limit the extent to which costs can be externalized and profits maximized. (The newfound prominence of these approaches could also be explained by the influence of campaign financing.) Equally unfortunate, there may be a limit to the endurance of principled, poorly compensated, and in many ways altruistic citizens. The emergence of these programs is more likely the result of a combination of these factors than of a common belief in the benefits of such efforts.

The proposed shift toward participatory decision making, which Sabel, Fung, and Karkkainen hail as an improvement while admitting it is improbable, stands as a rejection of laws designed for the common good, and a shift away from compensating stewards of the common good. At the same time, it preserves, and even expands, the rights of corporations and individuals to externalize costs in pursuit of profit. They suggest that this concept is counterintuitive. Its environmental benefits also are highly questionable. After hundreds of years of environmental degredation on our finite planet, where the impact of population growth and resource extraction are becoming ever more clear, our hard-won regulatory system should be allowed to work.

FRONTYARD PROPAGANDA

THEODORE J. LOWI

Sabel, Fung, and Karkkainen argue that we will come closer
to a maximum of environmental protection if we opt for a
nationally coordinated localism rather than the traditional
environmental regulation involving "hierarchical forms, in
which subordinate parts answer to the center's authority of
command." Everyone lives happily ever after within a new
structure that is a "collaborative and mutual accountability
of center to parts, parts to center, parts to other parts, all to
the whole enterprise—and to the public generally." Yet in
the very same paragraph, they inform us that their construct
is neither voluntarism—abdication of public authority to
private actors—nor is it devolution of authority from center
to local units. Rather, the center "ensures that local units live
up to their commitments." In other words, local interests,
including experts as well as amateurs, NIMBY groups and
selfless citizen groups, and of course the special-interest
groups and corporations interact in "a new form of democracy" to set "minimum performance standards [and] desirable targets"—then the standards they set through their
participation and interaction (rules? ordinances? policies?
directives?) would be enforced by that very same "authoritative command" of central government, of whose absence we

had just been assured. All this is affectionately referred to as a "rolling-rule regime," which means we can have our central government and reject it too.

This is where I came in, thirty-five years ago, in my confrontation with the late New Deal policies and the very same squaring-of-the-circle we confront in this piece. Words and style are different, because the underlying ideology (that is, the choir in wich Sabel, Fung, and Karkkainen are singing) is different. Their choir is the decadent phase of classical liberalism, whereas the choir in the 1960s was the decadent phase of social-democratic liberalism. But the motivation is the same—to try to finesse the coercive nature of public authority in order to validate, or embrace, or make more convincing the key principle of that ideology as it goes into decline. I'd call it ideology if the singers were unaware of the meaning of the song they were singing: I called it propaganda in my title because it seems to me to be an ideology of whose meaning Sabel, Fung, and Karkkainen are quite aware. The key principle of the classical liberal, laissez-faire ideology is that free-market localism bordering on anarchy is the best way to serve the public interest. Again, pretend away public authority.

They then use case studies to give the impression of empirical support for their process. In the New Deal era, case studies were also a major means of illustrating and confirming the political system to which the liberals then were committed. Political scientists called this the analysis and presentation of "how democracy works," or "how the system functions"—as though it did in fact function successfully, due to the principles being embraced. But the trouble is, for every supporting case study there is almost inevitably an unsupportive case study.

The same problem with case studies is even more pressing here because of the essential problem of "area and power" or "area and authority." Environmental policies almost always exist in a geographic context considerably larger than the area or principality within whose jurisdiction or boundaries the policy applies. In the 1960s Mancur Olson crystallized the intractable problem of public goods and their spillover effect (first described by David Hume back in 1740). First, there is an incentive not to begin a project if the public or spillover benefits can be enjoyed by everyone in the vicinity regardless of what they contribute; they can go along as "free riders." Second, if the public or spillover effects are costs rather than benefits, there is an equally strong incentive or tendency to act in concert to displace as many of the costs on to other people in other communities and other principalities, near and far.

Because both costs and benefits spread to a larger geographic context, we are led inexorably to the conclusion that the larger and more inclusive principality must have a superior share of authority over all the backyard environmental policy decisions. Sabel, Fung, and Karkkainen tell us of the importance of "contextual intelligence," but they don't say what context and how (and how inclusively) it is to be defined. Hopeful, they simply say that in the process of participation "ordinary citizens would become quasi-experts by imitation." And they support their discovery of this natural and spontaneous acquisition of expertise with the experience of their case study on the Chesapeake Bay Program, in which "the program"—I assume the officials or their public relations people are speaking for the program—"explicitly equated participation with the emulation of expert knowledge." This is a new pedagogical method for human adult learning, copied from canines and chimpanzees, that specifically relevant and required expertise, as well as "conceptual intelligence" and "system-level learning," can be acquired through mimicry. How much time does this education-through-emulation take? My answer to that question is inspired by something I learned from Shaw a long time ago: democracy will fail, because there aren't enough evenings in the week!

Even more hopeful (or downright propagandistic) is their report on the Massachusetts case, which involved broadening a federal "right-to-know" law mandating that the thirty thousand private and government-run facilities that meet statutory size requirements publish estimates of the amount of around 650 chemicals that are transferred off-site or are routinely or accidentally released. In 1989, Massachusetts expanded on the federal requirements to include "use or generation of toxics in any stage of production." But while the Massachusetts law set the ambitious goal of 50 percent reduction by 1997 and provided for penalties for "willful" violations of the reporting requirements, it (like the federal program) provided no penalties for failure to act on the reduction plans. The goals were to be achieved by an "obligation for self-monitoring to induce firms and citizens to acquire information that reveals problems and possibilities for their solution."

On the basis of this program, and all the observed participation and emulation and spontaneously acquired knowledge, Sabel, Fung, and Karkkainen proceed to claim that there is "substantial evidence . . . that this apparatus works." In the five years between 1990 and 1995, they report that "the production-adjusted use of toxic chemicals fell by 20 percent in Massachusetts and the generation of toxic by-products by 30 percent." Meanwhile, "the responding firms were most enthusiastic."

There is no reason to doubt their claim that use of toxic chemicals fell by 20 percent and generation of toxic by-products declined by 30 percent. But there is no basis for their claim that these important results were produced by the backyard process they outlined. For example, during and before that five-year period, Massachusetts, especially the Boston metropolitan area, went through a period of rather serious deindustrialization. Massachusetts reached its peak growth in heavy industry or manufacturing in 1984, with close to 674,000 employees; it then declined by mid-1999 to 435,000. That 35 percent decline was bad news for the "Massachusetts miracle," but good news for Massachusetts breathers, with the closing of some of those old, first-generation factories. Meanwhile, the city of Boston was losing population and the Boston metropolitan area (as defined by the U.S. Census Bureau) grew by a mere 0.8 percent, second to the bottom among the thirty major metropolitan areas in the United States. To attribute a 20 to 30 percent improvement in anything to a pussy-footed "rolling-rule regime" is no less a propaganda ploy than a president claiming credit for improvement in GDP or SAT, or a mayor claiming a personal victory over crime. And meanwhile, suburban and open country areas just beyond the Boston backyard in central Massachusetts, Connecticut, and Long Island are suffering with their highest ozone scores.

I am glad I took on the assignment of responding to their essay because I can see more clearly now than ever the insidious neoclassical liberal (Republican party) influence on the thinking of intelligent policy analysts and advocates. In that light I would like to end this with a couple of warnings, pedagogically speaking. First, never fall in love with process. Americans love process, especially if it is grounded in competition, visibility, and democracy. I suppose this is because it helps us maintain the appearance of consensus. But process is a double-edged sword: eventually it will cut the other way, and then it will be called betrayal.

Second, if we really want a safer and healthier environment we will either have to embrace drastic deindustrialization with a smaller-is-beautiful standard, or we will have to take our beloved process and place it in a solid, legal framework. You can set strict standards—regionally, nationally, internationally, as the situation warrants—and you put the burden of participation on the polluter. That standard can be a rule or a tax. It puts all interested parties on an equal plane, part of a stable and understandable structure. And it enables us to ask the truly operational question, which I heard Milton Friedman ask thirty years ago at one of the first conferences on the early environmental protection movement: How much pollution can we afford?

MODELS OF REINVENTION

DANIEL A. FARBER

Proposals to reinvent regulation are all the rage today. Perhaps the most vivid illustration is the transformation of the Endangered Species Act from a draconian ban on development to a flexible vehicle for ecosystem protection through habitat conservation plans. As Sabel, Fung, and Karkkainen document, such reinvention efforts are now being pursued with much energy and imagination at all levels of government, as well as in the private sector. It is clear what reinvention is designed to replace: a regime purportedly dominated by centralized regulation and punitive sanctions. Much less clear is precisely what reinvention means or how reinvention relates to the existing framework of environmental law.

At present, three different ways of thinking about reinvention are emerging in the environmental arena. Although we don't yet know the future of reinvention, it seems likely to lie somewhere in the triangle marked out by these three models. The first model, which is ably developed by Sabel, Fung, and Karkkainen, views reinvention as a multilateral process. This model eventually hopes to produce new, ecosystem-based governance structures. Another model is unilateral, focusing on the potential for self-regulation by firms. In this model, the government's primary role is catalyzing and enforcing rules designed by industry itself. The third model is bilateral. It focuses on bargaining between regulators and the regulated, with public-interest groups and others playing a secondary watchdog role. All these models highlight governance, self-regulation, or bargaining as the key feature of reinvention. In these models, or in some combination of them, we must seek the future of reinvention.

The governance model is the most exciting, since it promises not only efficient environmental regulation but also a rebirth of participatory democracy. Sabel, Fung, and Karkkainen see the seeds of this model in some existing programs such as habitat conservation plans or the new watershed planning efforts for the Chesapeake and San Francisco Bay Areas. Although this model may have genuine transformative potential, there are also serious risks in switching from existing governance structures. While existing structures are imperfect, they have been honed over time. The new governance structures that Sabel, Fung, and Karkkainen advocate pose a host of unresolved questions about the representativeness of participants, the accountability of governments and others, and the incentives for all of the parties to participate constructively.

These issues have yet to be resolved persuasively. As to the putative representatives of the public interest, we must wonder who will anoint them, what incentives and resources they will have to participate constructively, and how their performance will be assessed. (This has been a recurring and sometimes bitterly contested issue in the formation of habitat conservation plans.) How will the national interest in environmental quality be protected in a system that delegates effective management to the local level, and what will prevent a "race to the bottom" by local regions seeking economic advantages? After all, the reason we have federal environmental regulations such as the Clean Water Act is that the states weren't doing their jobs. And should we trust the "foxes"—the targets of regulation—to sit on the committee in charge of designing the proverbial henhouse? We risk recreating the pattern of previous generations of government regulation, where regulatory bodies like the Interstate Commerce Commission were dominated by the very industries they were supposed to be regulating. If we find answers to these questions, the governance model may prove transformative—but these answers will not be available overnight.

The self-regulation model, if anything, puts even more faith in taming the foxes so they will voluntarily help guard the henhouse. It's easy to be cynical about this approach; firms often seem to be more interested in minimizing their costs than in protecting the environment. But in recent studies, environmental economists have identified various incentives for firms to improve their environmental records, including pressure from customers, the desire to head off more rigorous regulation, and negative stock market reactions to environmental misconduct. And, as Sabel, Fung, and Karkkainen point out, there have been some impressive efforts at self-regulation by the nuclear industry, and in the wake of Bhopal by the chemical industry. There is also fairly persuasive evidence that disclosure laws, like California's extensive toxics disclosure rules, actually have a significant effect on the performance of industry. Still, it would take an exceptional degree of optimism to view self-regulation as the mainstay of environmental protection. All too often, harming the environment is good for profits, and even the best-intentioned business managers cannot ignore the ultimate reality of the balance sheet.

This leaves the bargaining model, which takes the existing regulatory scheme as a baseline and views reinvention as a way of negotiating from this baseline to outcomes that are better for both industry and environment. A simple example is provided by the EPA's program for Supplemental Environmental Projects (SEPs). A SEP allows a firm to avoid paying part of its fine for environmental violation by undertaking a project like cleaning up a local lake. This is a familiar process to lawyers, who are used to seeing similar forms of negotiation used every day to settle disputes. If we had complete trust in the federal government as a guardian of the public interest, we could be positive that the outcome of this process would be better for the environment (otherwise the government wouldn't agree) and better for the industry (otherwise the firm wouldn't agree). We could then celebrate a win-win solution. The problem is that we can't be completely confident of the government's ability and incentives—"capture" by industry is a familiar problem.

So we will need safeguards, probably including some involvement by public-interest groups. But designing these safeguards isn't easy. For instance, if involvement by public-interest groups is too extensive, the bargaining process may devolve into a form of the governance model. One option is to leave public-interest groups out of the initial bargaining process, but empower them to overturn the deal if it inadequately protects the environment.

Making the bargaining process work is a challenge, but it seems less audacious than trying to redesign the governance system or place all our trust on the goodwill of industry. At least in the short to medium term, conceptualizing reinvention as a form of bargaining, rather than as a novel form of governance or as self-regulation, seems to be the most useful way to move forward. But in the end, more will depend on the ability and imagination of the reinventors than on the conceptual frameworks of academics.

BUILDING CONSENSUS

LAWRENCE SUSSKIND

The partnerships that have caught the eye of Sabel, Fung, and Karkkainen do not just involve technical practitioners and citizens; they are collaborations among a wide range of stakeholders who realize that well-managed, face-to-face problem-solving sessions can help them advance their self-interest. While we can debate just how much of a democratic reform these activities represent, they certainly have produced impressive environmental results.[1] Indeed, the "improbable reorientation" that Sabel, Fung, and Karkkainen have discovered has been going on for quite some time under the broader banner of the environmental dispute resolution movement. There are literally hundreds of instances in which large numbers of people representing a wide range of contending groups have, with the help of trained mediators, worked out voluntary agreements, including performance standards to which all parties (including the public agencies) have agreed to be bound. In fact, there are even federal and state laws encouraging (and circumscribing) such consensus-building efforts as well as university programs that offer all relevant groups the knowledge and skills needed to participate in these negotiations.

Because Sabel, Fung, and Karkkainen are not attentive to the full range of relevant experience, they focus on questions that practitioners in environmental dispute resolution have already resolved, and they don't get to the next set of questions on which we need their help. In particular, they are musing about three things that have, for better or worse, been resolved: the relationship between the power that seemingly devolves to ad hoc assemblies in this new form of regulatory dialogue, and the formal decision-making authority that has always been in the hands of regulatory agencies; the role of experts versus the role of less-engaged citizens who are not formally included in discussions; and, finally, the potential split among environmental activists into those who "prefer the inside game of pluralist grappling for influence at power centers" and those who are "reorganizing to take advantage of the local participatory possibilities of the emergent regime." I will summarize how these issues have been resolved and spell out the next set of questions that require attention.

Some Settled Questions

1. Power and Authority. When a legislative body enacts a law (and an administrative agency adopts rules to implement that law), the agencies involved cannot turn over to an ad hoc assembly the authority to set performance standards or other terms of enforcement on a case-by-case basis. What they can do, though, is ask an appropriately selected set of stakeholders to generate a proposal (that is, a set of consensus recommendations) that is not inconsistent with the intent of the relevant law and regulations. While the agency retains the power to ignore the group's advice, there is usually no reason for it to do so, especially if agency staff has participated at every stage of the consensus-building effort. Ad hoc consultations must take place "in the open," as required by open meeting or other sunshine laws. The product of most such collaborative partnerships are recommendations that still require the relevant agency to act. What is most interesting is that many of the negotiated outcomes of these ad hoc processes require members of the regulated community to accept constraints or to make voluntary commitments that exceed what the regulators could otherwise impose. They are accepted in exchange for flexibility in how and when certain regulatory requirements must be met.

2. *Experts and Expertise.* Most environmental dispute resolution efforts begin with a period of joint fact-finding. That is, all the stakeholders (including the regulators) agree on the selection of a set of experts to advise them collectively. Whatever knowledge and skills the experts have to offer are shared simultaneously with all the parties. A neutral facilitator acts as interlocutor, making sure that even the least technically skilled participant is clear about what the experts have to say and how they went about gathering information, making forecasts, and preparing analyses of various kinds. Thus, the technical resources operate in support of the collaborative effort—avoiding the "battle of the

printout" and the "dueling experts" so typical of legal confrontations.[2]

3. A Schism in the Environmental Community. Some advocacy groups have refused to participate in certain efforts to mediate environmental disputes, relying on media campaigns, direct action, and legal challenges to pursue their interests. Others have been willing to "come to the table" and have been remarkably successful at getting their way. Some advocacy groups have agreed to negotiate on some issues while refusing to do so on others. The same, I might add, is true of regulatory agencies. In some regions of the country, the Environmental Protection Agency has taken the lead in suggesting mediation, in other regions there have been few such efforts.

Whatever their reasons, the leaders reserve the right to decide whether or not to participate in particular consensus-building efforts. If a key player refuses to participate, then dispute resolution cannot go forward. As it turns out, though, there are usually more than enough disputants willing to negotiate. Since the product of these efforts is, again, only a proposal, and all such negotiations are transparent, groups that choose to stay on the sidelines retain an opportunity to make their views known at the end. Indeed, from a legal perspective, even those who choose to participate in an ad hoc effort to achieve a tailored settlement reserve their right to challenge the outcome in court if they feel they were deceived or that some constitutional questions remain unanswered.

THE QUESTIONS THAT REMAIN

After more than twenty years of experimentation and hundreds of documented successes, several important questions remain about environmental dispute resolution: Do mediated solutions have precedential value? Should the practice of environmental mediation be regulated? Does fairness require that hard-to-represent interests (like future generations) be represented by proxies?

1. Precedential Value. The point of case-by-case problem solving is to permit stakeholders to work out the most effective way of meeting the performance requirements contained in laws and regulations, and to stop mandating the choice of technology and other methodological details. It would follow, therefore, that differently tailored solutions might well emerge in roughly similar situations.

Our system of law and regulation presumes, however, that similar situations ought to be handled in the same way to ensure fairness. Whether procedural guarantees (like the right to participate in any mediated negotiation in which you are a stakeholder) will be sufficient to assure fair treatment remains to be seen. At present, mediated results are not recorded in the way legal decisions are. They can't be cited with the same effect in subsequent similar situations. Does fairness require that the results of environmental mediation ought to have precedential value?

2. Regulating the Mediators? There is a growing pool of experienced environmental mediators in the United States.

Various states and federal agencies maintain rosters of such professionals. But there is no certification by any central body. Mediators have very different levels of scientific background and mediation experience. Some are lawyers while others are not. One unanswered question is whether there is a minimum level of competence that should be required of anyone who proposes to mediate an environmental dispute.

3. Representation. There are almost always hard-to-represent or diffuse constituencies which are not formally represented in an environmental dispute resolution effort. One view is that representative democracy is not perfect, either, and that ad hoc efforts to resolve environmental disputes should not be held to a higher standard of "representativeness" than typical legislative or administrative procedures. The contrary view is that a system for selecting proxy representatives would not be hard to generate and would add to the democratic appeal of the new environmental regime.

Consensus building in environmental regulation requires (1) convening the appropriate parties, (2) clarifying roles and responsibilities appropriate to the situation, (3) deliberating in a transparent and effective way, (4) reaching and testing the scope of agreement, and (5) binding the parties to their commitments.[3] As Sabel, Fung, and Karkkainen suggest, when this is done right, "disciplined consideration of alternative policies leads protagonists to discover unanticipated solutions provisionally acceptable to all." This is true and important, but it is not news. The hard questions remain.

THE WESTERN EXPERIENCE

JASON F. SHOGREN

Sabel, Fung, and Karkkainen have seen the future of environmental policy, and it is local control through consensus with added accountability. Many people would like this view of the future, especially those in the rural interior West. Local resource control is an old idea that westerners have long advocated to the powers back East. Those who live here know the land, and have a vested interest in its care. And just as we are accountable to the land, we are accountable to one another, and to the nation. Working together to find common ground just makes common sense, which is why collaborative decision making flourishes. Collaboration groups now number in the hundreds, ranging from informal grassroots gatherings to government-mandated advisory councils.

This western vision is a driving force behind Enlibra, the Western Governors Association's new doctrine for environmental management in the region. The governors want less remote control and more local control over resources. Enlibra outlines their push for strong local leadership to balance development and conservation goals and resolve environmental conflicts. In fact, the first two principles of Enlibra are identical to the policy architecture promoted by Sabel, Fung, and Karkkainen.

The first Enlibra principle is "national standards, neighborhood solutions—assign responsibilities at the right level." Locals understand local conditions. Instead of offering unimaginative bureaucratic responses, the federal government should help local people and policy makers develop their own plans to achieve binding targets, and to provide accountability. The second principle is "collaboration, not polarization—use collaborative processes to break down barriers and find solutions." The western governors believe that community-based collaboration can help produce creative solutions with political momentum. Together these principles support local leadership and collaborative efforts to help landowners and others enhance the environment and achieve economic productivity. Sound familiar?

The western governors take this doctrine a few steps further. Enlibra does not hold fast to one tool as the means for effective and accountable local control of natural resources. Consensus works in some cases, but not in others. The program recognizes that a variety of tools in combination with collaboration can be used to improve environmental and community well-being. "Markets before mandates—pursue economic incentives whenever appropriate" is the relevant principal. In some cases, collaboration might be better organized with an auction block than at a bargaining table.

To illustrate, consider collaborative habitat conservation

plans (HCPs) designed to protect endangered species. Recall that an HCP acts as a safety valve for a private landowner whose property shelters an endangered species. A landowner with an approved HCP has a permit allowing the taking of endangered wildlife incidental to any otherwise lawful activity. The takings, however, cannot appreciably diminish the odds for survival and recovery of the species, and must be minimized and mitigated to the maximum extent practicable.

But at least three problems arise with the promotion of just consensus for HCPs—the scope has changed with time, the process might be manipulated, and the process is seen as an invasion of privacy. First, back in 1982, people promoting HCPs had in mind a single landowner affecting a single species. Today people use HCPs to cover thousands of landowners and hundreds of species. Collaboration efforts are often fragile, slow, tedious processes. And most mediators will admit that adding more stakeholders will increase the costs and decrease the productivity of collaborative efforts. Second, many urban environmentalists fear that slick industry dandies will dominate the bargaining with local rubes. They fear that savvy, trained experts with unending financial resources will pressure local communities to water down the HCP. The common perception is that anything so attractive to corporations and developers must be flawed.

Third, many private landowners do not want to participate in an HCP collaborative process because they see it as inherently unfair. They consider the HCP process as an invasion of their privacy, a slap at their stewardship efforts, and an unfair restriction on their ability to protect their investment. These landowners won't even enter into a discussion when the topic of an HCP process arises. Accepting the idea of a collaborative process for critical habitat protection could be interpreted as meaning that they are not taking good care of the land already. The old adages that "no good deed goes unpunished" and "give an inch, take a mile" capture their mood.

But getting the cooperation of private landowners is vital to the preservation of endangered species. About half of the listed endangered species have 80 percent of their habitat on private land. The question is what tool besides an HCP might work to induce proactive measures to protect endangered species on private property. The scheme would need to respect landowners' privacy, acknowledge their prior stewardship efforts, and allow some flexibility in how they protect their investments.

This big sticking item is compensation. Compensation for landowners has supporters and critics from both sides of the debate. Conservationists who support compensation see it as a practical way to buy cooperation; proponents among landowners argue that it is only fair to compensate property owners who are restricted in their ability to protect their investment. Conservationists who oppose compensation see it as a backdoor policy to sabotage the ESA through underfunding; averse landowners see compensation as a lever that will open the door for more federal control over their property, especially given the line of species being considered for listing.

A tool that might bring both sides together could be the creation of a market for critical habitat. Markets allow for both collaboration and privacy. While we might not be sitting across the table, a market exchange still implies a consensus. You want to buy habitat, I want to sell it. Landowners can be provided the opportunity to sell private shares of critical habitat rights on the open market without opening themselves up to public access. Sabel, Fung, and Karkkainen discount market-based solutions because they require too much information. This is a good point. But markets respect privacy, and can help overcome major constraints facing consensus.

After all, collaborative efforts face real constraints if explicit consensus is required. A shared feature of most models of consensus building is to even out power imbalances by "sharing information." But landowners who do not want to share information for whatever reason have little incentive to sit down and cooperate at the bargaining table. A market for critical habitat, on the other hand, would be similar to the real estate market. Private sector bioeconomic appraisers would assess the biological quality of the critical habitat rights offered up for sale. The appraiser would certify the habitat quality: four-star, three-star, and so on. Sellers would then post their offer to sell a given habitat right for a given price, subject to private appraisal. Negotiating fair market value for habitat rights would require independent and confidential biological and economic appraisals of habitat. Duration of the contract would be negotiated. Inspections and nonperformance could be standard rules or open for discussion. Most important, information not essential for the public enforcement of the transaction would remain confidential. There will be challenges. Finding landowners willing to sell habitat rights would be a task. Deciding where and how money should be spent to get the biggest ecological bang for the buck will take energy. Conservation contracts will have to be well specified because property rights (especially water rights) are often complicated. And determining which acquisition option is best for the circumstances—lease, purchase, or donation—must be thought through. This is not a pie-in-the-sky idea. Environmental markets are used around the globe and are being proposed for use in climate change as a cost-effective mechanism to get more environmental quality at lower cost. Such a market would complement or replace already existing programs that use bilateral negotiation, landowner by landowner.

Healthy local control in exchange for stricter accountability is a trade-off many westerners might make. Suggesting that consensus is the only means to prevent hapless parochialism, however, might be asking too much. There is no universally preferred tool. Sometimes consensus works, but other times incentives work better. The search for Enlibra, East or West, requires that we use the best tool for the task at hand.

CONSEQUENCES?

CASS R. SUNSTEIN

The intriguing and highly original discussion by Sabel, Fung, and Karkkainen points to an apparently new development, or set of developments, in the area of environmental regulation, with many promising features. But I am not sure that they have presented a compelling case that these developments are desirable. To answer that question it is necessary to know more, especially about the consequences for environmental protection.

A system of environmental protection might be evaluated either substantively or procedurally. Let us understand a substantive evaluation to involve an assessment of the system's contribution to overall well-being, which might be defined in many different ways. Well-being could, for example, involve utilitarian or economic considerations; it may or may not be limited to the well-being of human beings; it may or may not involve judgments about rights. Let us understand a procedural evaluation to involve not the product of the system but its legitimacy, to be assessed above all by reference to democratic considerations, which might also be understood in many different ways. The problem with Sabel, Fung, and Karkkainen's presentation is that we do not know that the developments they describe are contributing a great deal to the various substantive goals of environmental protection, nor do they warrant approval on procedural, democratic grounds.

A little background. Until the late 1960s, much (not all) of environmental protection in the United States occurred via private lawsuits and judge-made common law. The result was a system that, by this time, was plainly producing excessive levels of pollution, with extremely harmful effects to social well-being (defined in any reasonable way). As we now know, regulation could greatly reduce those harmful effects, not costlessly, but without introducing comparably large harmful effects. The common law system was also highly objectionable on democratic grounds, since it ensured that pollution levels would be set, not through accountable institutions, and not as a result of democratic deliberation, but by unelected judges.

Between 1970 and the present, much (not all) of environmental protection has occurred via a remarkably ambitious, complex, and cumbersome system of national regulation. In many ways, the substantive results have been excellent, with extraordinary decreases, for example, in concentrations of all of the major air pollutants; ambient concentrations of lead alone have decreased by about 80 percent since 1985. Common law judges have been replaced by far more democratic institutions. But there have been serious problems as well. Much of the national effort has shown poor priority setting, with some small problems receiving disproportionate attention, and with some large problems being neglected. For example, government devotes excessive attention to the relatively small problem of abandoned hazardous waste sites, and far too little attention to the much larger problem of indoor air pollution. Post-1970s environmentalism has also involved excessive costs, mostly because of the use of rigid, "command and control" regulation. Smarter and more flexible alternatives (such as taxes on polluting activities and tradable emissions rights) could have produced the same reductions with hundreds of millions and probably billions of dollars in savings—savings that might have been used for environmental or other purposes.

At the same time, the post-1970s environment process has been nothing to celebrate from the democratic point of view. Far from reflecting the deliberative judgments of the nation's citizenry, many governmental decisions have resulted from the political influence of well-organized private groups, such as the high-sulfur eastern coal lobby (attempting to use environmental protection to insulate itself from competition from low-sulfur western coal) and the corn lobby (attempting to promote ethanol).

An important question is whether the United States will be able to develop structures of environmental protection that better promote our substantive and procedural ideals. Recent initiatives, involving cost-benefit analysis and economic incentives, have accomplished considerable good—with cost-benefit analysis pointing the way toward aggressive initiatives to remove lead from gasoline and to control destruction of the ozone layer, and with economic incentives contributing to massive, low-cost reductions in acid deposition. But Sabel, Fung, and Karkkainen believe that they have identified much better, and largely unnoticed, structures for environmental protection, emerging from the participatory efforts of multiple actors and reducing key problems in flexible ways that do not impose an informational overload on national actors. There is a great deal of value in what they have to say; but from their discussion here, it remains unclear if the various initiatives—assuming that they amount to something like a unitary trend—deserve approval on either procedural or substantive grounds.

Democracy first: Sabel, Fung, and Karkkainen emphasize the involvement of many "local actors," but much of what they say is quite abstract. Do the emerging structures really promote democratic ideals, suitably specified? They might show instead compromises among a set of organized interests, local and national, rather than anything deliberative or democratic. To be sure, they identify far more participatory structures than national institutions are by themselves capable of providing, and the gain in local participation seems to be a large improvement. But surely many people are left out. Who are they, and with what consequences? Skeptics might fear that some of these processes are a form of environmental corporatism, reflecting not the outcomes of deliberative judgments of the citizenry, but negotiated solutions among visible well-organized actors. I doubt that the skeptics would be right, but it would be good for Sabel, Fung, and Karkkainen to dispel their fears, by specifying the relevant democratic ideal and by showing, in concrete terms, how the emerging processes comply with (and perhaps inform) it. The more important gap involves substance. What are the concrete results of the initiatives described by Sabel, Fung, and Karkkainen for social well-being, defined in any reasonable way? As an illustration, consider the Toxic Release Inventory, a program that does appear to be a terrific success story, spurring large decreases in toxic releases without national regulatory controls. To make a full evaluation, it would be desirable—indeed, it would seem indispensable—to know both the costs of these decreases and the benefits for human health and welfare (and for nonhuman animals as well). By themselves reductions are surely good, but it is impossible to know how good they are without having a sense of the consequences of exposure for what we do or should care about. If the reductions have done very little to improve human health, but have increased prices or decreased wages, the program is nothing to celebrate.

So too for the reductions brought about in Massachusetts. Sabel, Fung, and Karkkainen say that "this apparatus works" because it has brought about substantial reductions in toxic chemicals and also "enabled firms to discover significant net benefits of pollution prevention." Net benefits in terms of what, concretely speaking? Do we know that the reductions have had good effects for social well-being, suitably defined? Would more reductions be better? Have the current reductions produced (1) trivial, (2) moderate, or (3) large benefits for health? It seems impossible to evaluate the program without knowing the answers to such questions. Similar issues might be raised about the Responsible Care initiative and also the Chesapeake Bay Program. Compare the "best available technology" requirement in national environmental law, a requirement that has undoubted popular appeal but that has proved crude and troublesome partly because, from the standpoint of human health and other substantive values, some companies should do less than to use the best available technology, and others should do more— by, for example, scaling back operations when the health consequences of even the best technology is serious.

This is not at all to say that a substantive evaluation of environmental programs should depend on a crudely economistic cost-benefit analysis; surely it should not. But from what Sabel, Fung, and Karkkainen say, it is possible that the health and associated benefits of the reductions are small or even trivial and also that the resulting decreases have been quite costly (even if in a sense voluntary). Costs of this kind are no mere technical matter; their consequences may include reduced employment, increased poverty, and increased prices, which come down especially hard on those least able to pay. Or it is possible that the relevant programs have done relatively little in terms of promoting the substantive goals of environmental protection—and that other approaches would be better. Most of all, we need to know more about the effects of these programs for the health and welfare values associated with the relevant programs.

To deepen the account of the emerging structure, it would be helpful to have more in the way of both theory and empirical work. What is the account of democratic legitimacy by which we might evaluate the structures described here, and do those structures fit that account? By what substantive criteria might we assess a system for environmental protection and how, concretely, have the structures at issue done under that standard? Have they, for example, reduced serious risks to life and health without imposing high costs, which can lead to lower wages, less employment, and higher prices? It is not the least virtue of this intriguing essay that the developments they describe put such questions squarely on the table.

3

REPLY

CHARLES SABEL, ARCHON FUNG,
AND BRADLEY KARKKAINEN

In "Beyond Backyard Environmentalism," we argue that a new form of decentralized but coordinated environmental regulation is successfully addressing a surprisingly broad range of apparently intractable problems. Even more improbably, its success depends on a new and potentially wide-ranging form of directly deliberative democratic participation.

Our respondents range from enthusiasts to skeptics. They share a sincere and incisive engagement with fundamental issues; for this we thank them. In general, their doubts concern either the feasibility of the rolling-rule regime that we describe, or its normative desirability. Of those who question its feasibility, some deny that it is workable at all, while others view it as a limited adjunct to the existing regulatory regime. Those who raise normative questions ask us for a more fully developed theory of the democratic underpinnings of backyard environmentalism. They wonder how one could know that backyard environmentalism, even if fully realized, would more accurately reflect the desires of citizens, or better translate those desires into effective policy than the current regime.

Feasibility

The most vociferous critics of feasibility dismiss the alternative as "wishful thinking" (Jacqueline Savitz), or, more harshly, as the have-your-cake-and-eat-it-too "propaganda" of the "decadent phase of classical liberalism" (Theodore Lowi). So anxious are they to prove the impossibility of the regime we describe that they would deny the underlying facts. But if there are facts that counter our claims, they have not found them. Thus Lowi attributes Massachusetts' apparent progress in toxics use reduction to large-scale deindustrialization. But the record amply documents otherwise: production-adjusted use and emissions of toxic substances have fallen dramatically under the TURA, both in the aggregate and for individual firms and facilities. Similarly, Savitz characterizes documented reductions in toxic emissions under the TRI as the mere by-product of conventional regulation, in particular the ban on CFCs, combined with "paper reductions" produced by changes in estimation methods. In fact, CFCs represent only a small fraction of the TRI pollutants, and even discounting for paper reductions, the TRI emissions have fallen deeply and across-the-board for virtually all listed substances, well beyond levels demanded by regulatory standards (where they exist at all), in virtually every industrial sector.

But we don't rest our case on the factual errors of our respondents. We are confident that the successes of backyard environmentalism are not wholly imaginary, in part because we are far from alone in recognizing them. Thus, while concerned about practical limits and transition paths, DeWitt John and Dan Fiorino take it as given that in crucial respects the new architecture has already been demonstrated in practice. Both are close observers of emerging regulatory trends and active participants in debates concerning the posed alternatives. So while they are fallible, they are not likely to confuse academic bombast for practical innovation. Similarly, we agree with Jason Shogren, who argues that the collaborative model will be no news at all to his fellow westerners, for whom it is already commonplace.

Finally, Lawrence Susskind, drawing from his broad professional experience as a master practitioner of Alternative Dispute Resolution (ADR), takes it for granted that parties holding contrary views might, through practical deliberation and exchange of views, transcend their fixed understandings to reach mutually acceptable solutions. This capacity to innovate in the midst of conflict is surely among the most counterintuitive requirements of the new regime. (While in this sense ADR is an important precursor of the regime we propose, we disagree with Susskind's view that a comprehensive alternative could emerge from the myriad of discrete local ADR decisions, if only those decisions had precedential character. Despite its broad accomplishments, ADR has remained peripheral to the reform of public administration, in part because it has no notion of how the center might be transformed to reflect, learn from, and guide the successes of local practical deliberation.)

A deeper challenge to our view is the contention of several critics that the new architecture is feasible, but only narrowly so, insofar as it has proved useful and practicable only in exceptional circumstances, and then only given the continuing backdrop of conventional regulation. From this perspective, the phenomenon we describe may never amount to more than tinkering at the margins of the established regime. The core of this view is that effective regulation depends on state coercion that is inherent in the current regime but absent from our architecture. Some of our critics believe in addition that the current system is less rigid and more extensible to new circumstances than we credit. At the limit, this leads to Daniel Farber's claim that correcting the current regime through bilateral negotiation between regulators and private parties is preferable to our "multilateral" approach. Others appear to agree with our characterization of the limits of the current regime, but see our participatory remedy as so demanding as to be unworkable in most circumstances. We consider these objections in turn.

As we argue in "Beyond Backyard Environmentalism," we fully agree that coercion is indispensable to effective regulation. Even where there are long-term, mutually beneficial solutions to regulatory disputes, self-interested parties would be tempted to sacrifice broad and long-term gains for narrow and short-term benefits unless deterred by credible threats of penalties. The dispute with our critics, then, turns on whether the necessary coercion can only be supplied by the current fixed-rule regime, or whether our rolling-rule alternative can provide it better.

For an illustration, consider again the evolution of habitat conservation planning. Without the coercive threat of the Endangered Species Act, there would have been no HCPs. In this sense, the emergence of the new regime depended upon the coercion of the old. Effective HCPs, however, establish locally contextualized coercive regimes of their own: developers who fail to comply with requirements of the habitat regime, whether or not these are connected to the fate of a listed species, lose the right to develop. These regimes form a kind of halfway house between the status quo and a full-fledged alternative. But is it true, as the critics seem to suggest, that the construction of local HCPs can be triggered only by waiver from a fixed (and draconian) uniform rule like the ESA? We think not. To be sure, strong incentives, positive or negative, will be necessary to secure the cooperation of landowners.

But imagine a congressionally sanctioned alternative regime in which participation in a local HCP is compulsory (and subject to stiff penalties for noncompliance) wherever habitats are judged to be in serious decline. That determination, in turn, would be made under processes and standards that are themselves not fixed, but continuously improving with the experience and learning generated by the HCP program itself. This bootstrapping alternative would obviate the need for fixed regulation and establish in its stead a full-scale rolling-rule regime. In this progression, we shift from one coercive regime to another without ever passing through a phase in which regulation depends on voluntary compliance.

We think, unsurprisingly, that those who advocate the extension of the current regime rather than construction of an alternative overstate its adaptability and the persistence of its core principles in the face of such change as does occur. Two kinds of evidence weigh against the preference for extension over renovation. First, reformers developed unconventional approaches like the Chesapeake Bay Program, the TRI, and TURA to address the biggest and most complex problems—ecosystem decline, nonpoint-source pollution, and toxic pollutants—outside the existing regimes precisely because extension of the existing rules proved unworkable. Moreover, even in cases like HCPs, where rules were extended and made flexible through processes that are arguably related to those described by Farber, the underlying regime was reoriented rather than stabilized. HCPs make the ESA "work," but only at the cost of raising deep questions about whether the ESA is the right way to conserve habitats in the first place.

On the question of whether the degree of participation that we observe is limited to the described instances, caution is in order, but false certainties about alleged limits are not. Participation in the cases we present already exceeds what the most skeptical critics would have thought possible under any circumstances. It is a general and understandable pessimism, and not any well-founded theory of what citizens can do, that drives them to conclude that the limits of participation have been reached with these successes. We are not blind to the dismal history of popular participation in the many forums of representative democracy, nor do we think that participation can come for free in any imaginable democratic regime. However, experience with the institutions of backyard environmentalism reveals unexpectedly deep deliberative capacities among a surprisingly broad range of the citizenry. A great advantage of our experimentalist program is that it can be built incrementally. Each step places greater demands on citizens and proceeds until the limits of participation have been demonstrably reached. This way, institutional practice disciplines democratic optimism without allowing reform to be prematurely truncated by untested and unfounded skepticism.

Democracy?

Now to the normative concerns. On what conception of democracy should backyard environmentalism count as democratic, let alone more so than the current regime? Relatedly, to use Cass Sunstein's terms, does it out perform—either procedurally or substantively—that which already exists? These are, of course, vast and crucial questions. Here we can do little more than name an alternative theory that might be elaborated to explain the democratic character of backyard environmentalism and that might begin to address the question of its comparative performance.

The background view of democracy that informs the views of many of our critics is, broadly speaking, Madisonian. Power is parceled among separate branches of government. Deliberation—preference-changing reflection in the service of the public interest—is the province of a political or administrative elite buffered from everyday concerns. Citizens participate primarily on Election Day by passing summary judgments on the large choices made by their representatives. Whatever its failings, this system generates large outcomes that reflect citizens' preferences, and protects their liberties. The alternative view underpinning our environmental proposal is another, directly deliberative variant of Madisonianism. First, in place of deliberation at a distance, it emphasizes the capacity of practical problem-solving activity to reveal new possibilities and thus to open the way for solutions that are different from both the ideal of elite deliberation and the reality of interest-group dealing. Second, where Madisonians rely on the separation of powers, this alternative harnesses a deliberative competition among institutions to ensure that they all act in the public interest. Thus, on the expanded version of HCPs we envision, the practice of other HCPs would provide a rich pool of information and comparative standards against which to hold local jurisdictions accountable in regard both to substantive performance outcomes and their respect for democratic procedure (for instance, whether they are as representative as practice shows that they can be).

While this directly deliberative form of democracy may respond to the desires of actors locally, the general decisions it frames may not reflect the preferences of citizens in the aggregate. Thus Sunstein wonders whether the regime we envision may result in radical over- or underregulation—or perhaps both simultaneously, by overregulating in trivial areas while failing to address more important problems that arise on a larger scale. The issue is important, but he overlooks the possibilities for addressing this problem in the neo-Madisonian framework.

A central theme of our argument throughout has been that it is impossible to attain the panoptic knowledge required by the Madisonian ideal. Recall the repeated failure of large-scale studies in the Chesapeake Bay Program to generate definitive answers to the problems of that ecosystem. In the face of this impossibility, the new regime institutionalizes mechanisms for monitored experimentation, learning, and continuous improvement at both local and aggregate levels. HCPs, for example, pair developers concerned with overregulation with environmentalists concerned with underregulation to develop plans and monitoring regimes that generate rich and continuous flows of information, correct errors, revise targets, and adjust means as conditions change and new information emerges. Local results are compared against one another so that parochial and hasty judgments about the feasibility of regulation will be checked by the full range of experience. Without such fine-grained information, how can there be effective decisions about allocation of regulatory resources among environmental and other purposes?

The decisions that emerge from these searches cannot pretend to be globally optimal. Nonetheless, they should over time result in a vast improvement in our information about the choices we face and their costs. Ironically, then, by abandoning the pretension to comprehensive knowledge supposed by traditional cost-benefit analysis and related deliberative ideals, backyard environmentalism may generate a far richer canvas of our possibilities, and their relative prices, than we could otherwise have.

Backyard environmentalism, in both theory and practice, has a long way to go before making good on these promises. But in crucial areas it has already delivered more than the traditional institutions of representative democracy are able to supply. To progress further it will have to overcome the limits its critics have identified. For the sake of democracy, we hope it does.

NOTES

CHARLES SABEL, ARCHON FUNG, AND
BRADLEY KARKKAINEN / *Beyond Backyard Environmentalism*

1. The authors thank Craig Thomas for sharing his knowledge about the Coachella Valley Habitat Conservaton Plan's efforts in a personal communication as well as in Craig W. Thomas and Charles Schweik, "Regulatory Compliance Under the Endangered Species Act: A Time-Series Analysis of Habitat Conservation Planning." See also Robert Thompson, "The Coachella Valley Habitat Conservation Plan," in Judith Innes et al., *Coordinating Growth and Environmental Management Through Consensus Building* (Berkeley: University of California Press, 1994): 211–31.

2. The two measures are the number of "scrams," or rapid reactor shutdowns, and the number of safety system actuations. Both represent a gauge of the frequency of emergencies and are therefore inversely correlated with overall reactor safety. Between 1980 and 1990, the number of scrams per unit decreased by 80 percent. The number of safety system actuations decreased by 60 percent between 1985 (the first year such measures were taken) and 1990.

3. 50 C.F.R. 17.3. The Supreme Court has upheld this regulation as a valid interpretation of the statutory prohibition against "taking" of listed wildlife. See *Babbitt v. Sweet Home Chapter of Communities for a Great Oregon*, 115 SC 2407 (1995).

4. U.S. Fish and Wildlife Service, Division of Endangered Species, "Status of Habitat Conservation Plans" (April 23, 1999). This document can be obtained at http://www.fws.gov/r9endspp/hcp/hcptable.pdf.

5. John Kostyack, "Habitat Conservation Planning: Time to Give

Conservationists and Other Concerned Citizens a Seat at the Table," *Endangered Species UPDATE* 14 (July–August 1997): 51–55.

6. An effective system must be an adaptive one because even the best science gets better: "There is never enough information" to allow time-less determinations of fixed rules, and "[n]o key ecosystem management decision ever gets made in a setting of adequate information." See George Frampton, "Ecosystem Management in the Clinton Adminis-tration," *Duke Environmental Law and Policy Forum* 7 (1996): 39. Framp-ton was, at the time he wrote these words, assistant secretary for Fish, Wildlife, and Parks in the Department of the Interior, overseeing the Fish and Wildlife Service and its endangered species program.

7. In interviewing USFWS and Interior officials in July, 1998, we learned that no one in Washington had even collected the HCPs that had already been negotiated up until that point—much less read them, or at-tempted to absorb any generally applicable lessons that might be learned from them.

8. Peter Kareiva et al., *Using Science in Habitat Conservation Plans* (Santa Barbara: National Center for Ecological Analysis and Synthesis, 1998).

9. Frampton describes how the FWS's traditional emphasis on purely science-based decision making stands at odds with the inherently politi-cal nature of ecosystem management.

10. For a thoughtful and textured environmentalist critique of the shortcomings of public participation in HCP planning, see Kostyack, "Habitat Conservation Planning."

11. See *Federal Register* 64, no. 45 (March 9, 1999): 11488. A first draft of this database can be obtained on the Internet at http://www.fws.gov/r9endspp/hcp/hcptable.pdf.

12. See Lee P. Breckenridge, "Reweaving the Landscape: The Institu-tional Challenges of Ecosystem Management for Lands in Private Ownership," *Vermont Law Review* 19 (1995): 363.

13. See Kostyack, "Habitat Conservation Planning."

14. Tellingly, the Washington office of the National Wildlife Federa-tion made itself a central repository for habitat conservation plans before it occurred to anyone in the Department of the Interior that such a thing might be useful. In addition, NWF convened the first national confer-

ence to assess HCP policy and practice and has produced thoughtful and detailed critiques of many HCPs that will undoubtedly inform future ones.

JACQUELINE SAVITZ / *Compensating Citizens*

1. The Chemical Manufacturers' Association simultaneously touts Responsible Care and lobbies to weaken the TRI.
2. There are other examples. For instance, the benefits of the sulfur dioxide trading program were largely attributable to increased availability of low-sulfur coal.

LAWRENCE SUSSKIND / *Building Consensus*

1. See Lawrence Susskind, Paul Levy, and Jennifer Thomas-Larmer, *Negotiating Environmental Agreements* (San Francisco: Island Press, 1999).
2. See Connie Ozawa, *Recasting Science* (Boulder, Col.: Westview Press, 1991).
3. See Lawrence Susskind, Sarah McKearnan, and Jennifer Thomas-Larmer, *The Consensus Building Handbook* (Thousand Oaks, Calif.: Sage Publishers, 1999).

ABOUT THE CONTRIBUTORS

DANIEL A. FARBER is the Henry J. Fletcher Professor of Law at the University of Minnesota Law School. He has written extensively about environmental law, most recently in *Eco-Pragmatism: Making Sensible Environmental Decisions in an Uncertain World.*

DANIEL J. FIORINO directs the Emerging Strategies Division in the Office of Policy at the U.S. Environmental Protection Agency. He is the author of *Making Environmental Policy.*

ARCHON FUNG is assistant professor at the John F. Kennedy School of Government, Harvard University.

DEWITT JOHN directs the Center for the Economy and the Environment at the National Academy of Public Administration.

BRADLEY KARKKAINEN is associate professor at Columbia Law School.

THEODORE J. LOWI is the John L. Senior Professor of American Institutions at Cornell University.

CHARLES SABEL teaches law at Columbia University.

JACQUELINE SAVITZ is the executive director of Coast Alliance.

JASON F. SHOGREN is Stroock Distinguished Professor of Natural Resource Conservation and Management at the University of Wyoming. In 1997 he served as the senior economist for environmental and natural resource policy on the Council of Economic Advisers.

CASS R. SUNSTEIN teaches at the University of Chicago Law School. He is author, most recently, of *One Case at a Time* and (with Stephen Holmes) *The Cost of Rights.*

LAWRENCE SUSSKIND is Ford Professor of Urban and Environmental Planning at MIT and president of the Consensus Building Institute. He is the author (with Paul Levy and Jennifer Thomas-Larmer) of *Negotiating Environmental Agreements.*

ABOUT THE CONTRIBUTORS

ERIC WELTMAN was the program director of Toxics Action Center from 1995 through 1999. He is currently organizing and policy director for Citizens for Participation in Political Action (CPPAX).

MATTHEW WILSON has been the director of the Toxics Action Center since 1989. He has helped more than 150 neighborhood groups organize to fight toxics hazards in their communities.